THE SWEETER SIDE OF CANDIDA

DESSERTS FOR THE HOLIDAYS,

SPECIAL OCCASIONS,

& EVERYDAY SWEET TREATS

BY PAULA MILLER & SARAH IVES, *WHOLE INTENTIONS*

TABLE OF CONTENTS

THE APPENDIX

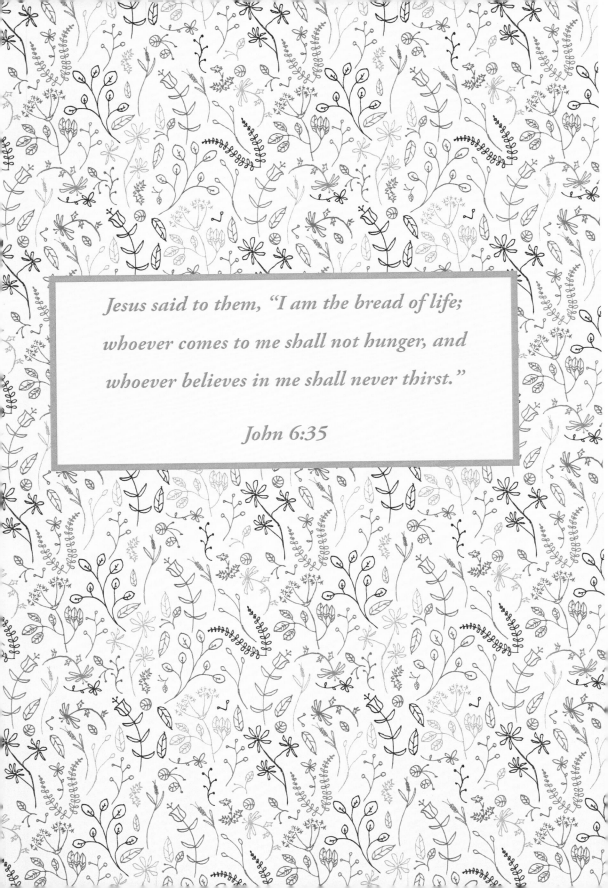

Jesus said to them, "I am the bread of life;
whoever comes to me shall not hunger, and
whoever believes in me shall never thirst."

John 6:35

COPYRIGHT

//

There are references to links in this book. For a full list of these links, please visit:

http://wholeintentions.com/tssc-book-links/

This cookbook is dedicated to Jesus, our Rock
and Redeemer.

We're two unworthy sinners, blessed beyond measure, and baking
for God's glory.

We have fought, and continue to fight, for our
own good health. It is our hope and prayer that
this cookbook encourages you and sweetens your
journey while battling candida.

PAULA'S STORY

Hi, I'm Paula. **Our candida journey, like most people's, started long before we realized it.** When my husband Travis and I were first married, we lived off Pasta-Roni, pizza, and liters of pop. It was a disgustingly carefree life. (The kids are so envious.)

But during our newly-wedded bliss and through the next seven or so years, Travis suffered strange health problems - and they were escalating. He tried to convince me he was allergic to me since they didn't start until after we were married. But, yeah - that didn't fly. He's totally doing the 'till death do us part'. ;)

We visited family doctors, emergency room doctors, and specialists. Eventually we **grew tired of them shrugging their shoulders and suggesting it was 'all in his head'**, so we began looking at alternative medicine and found a naturopath near us. Travis was diagnosed with Lyme Disease and candida.

Hearing "Lyme Disease" scared us to death. And **according to our naturopath, *everyone* had candida so we pretty much ignored it**. Instead we focused on the Lyme, going so far as to travel across the country to an alternative clinic for Lyme in 2008.

When you stick two country-bred adults with four kids in a one bedroom apartment in Reno, Nevada for six weeks, you're bound to have a photo albums worth of 'favorite memories'. Oh, yeah - precious times.

While at the Lyme clinic we learned Travis had food allergies, the main one being gluten, so we jumped headfirst into the gluten-free world. Between the clinic and the diet change, Travis's symptoms eased. . .for a while anyway.

Then we heard about the book Nourishing Traditions. After devouring it from cover to cover we realized that **just eating gluten-free wasn't the answer.** Further research told us that many of the foods we ate, (i.e. carbs, starches, and even natural sugars) were feeding a common and underestimated problem called. . .candida. Light bulb!

We started researching candida and what we discovered surprised us. If what we read was true, **nearly everything we were putting in our mouths was feeding the problem.** So we jumped online, found a candida diet that looked strict enough for a monk, and followed it 'somewhat' for about a year. I'll be honest though, it was pretty tough.

Though there were a few ups and downs, Travis did make progress. The turning point was about nine months into the diet when he walked in the house and stated, "I don't know what it is, but for the past few days I feel like a cloud has lifted off my brain. **I just. . .*feel* better."**

Since then I've come across several other candida diets, **but it wasn't until I found Dr. Bakker's ebook,** Candida Crusher**, that I felt like I'd found a thorough explanation of candida with a diet anyone could follow.**

Since then I've shared several emails with Dr. Bakker about his diet and with his permission, was able to share it in *Healing Candida With Food*, an eCookbook with over 130 of my favorite candida-allowed recipes.

Those tasty dishes sure hit the spot for family meals, and give new ideas for breakfast, lunch, and dinner. . .and this cookbook, created with my dear friend Sarah, is sure to **satisfy that sweet-tooth while still giving candida a boot out the door. :)**

If you have any questions about candida, this particular diet, or those memorable six weeks of family *togetherness*, you can visit my blog, Whole Intentions, or contact me via email at paula@wholeintentions.com.

His, by Grace alone,

Paula

SARAH'S STORY

I am so thrilled to be teaming up with Paula at <u>Whole Intentions</u> and to have had the opportunity to create this delightful cookbook with her. I've been a reader of her blog for quite some time and have learned so much from her. **We both have a heart for baking, helping people, and a love for the Lord that bonds us together.**

Probably the biggest thing that I learned from Paula though is that I have candida. Badly. So, I'm sharing my journey, at <u>Whole Intentions</u>, to health and fitness. But here, in *The Sweeter Side of Candida*, I'm hoping to share a piece of my heart! I love to bake, and cook, and text Paula random photos of decadent creations 50 times a day. **Like many of you, I'm facing a battle daily to get well, to get fit, and to get HEALTHY and I've been baking my way to wellness one cookie, cake, and smoothie at a time!**

Not only do I have candida, but also I've struggled with my weight and sin issues around food for as long as I can remember. As a child, I was on a tremendous amount of antibiotics, so I'm pretty sure the candida and the weight issues started close to the same time – around age 6 (and now I know you're dying to know – I'm 34 – yup, probably 28 years of this crazy stuff).

Anyone with candida knows it's HUNGRY!!! It must be fed to thrive and grow and yes, that means too much food, which often leads to excess fat.

Shortly after getting married 8 years ago, I reached the highest weight of my life at 215 lbs. I seriously can't believe how sad I look in photos from this period of my life. **I was so sick and had no idea what was ailing me.**

I'm just about 5'5", and well, at 215 I was really big, miserable, and sick as a dog. I gave up wheat, sugar, and dairy and lost 30 lbs in about 6 months.

Not too long after that I got pregnant with my first child. Once he was born, I joined one of the most popular diets in the country and lost another 25 lbs (from the 30 lbs. before), but honestly I was starving. I don't know how anyone can live on so little food (especially when it's all low fat – I mean seriously, **pass me the grass fed butter!**).

Luckily, I got pregnant and got off that crazy train. When baby #2 came along the weight didn't come off quite so quickly, and with baby #3 it was even worse (it wasn't budging at all). I found myself at about 30 lbs. over a healthy weight for my body.

During all these years I struggled with yeast infections, sinus infections, bladder infections, digestive issues, and on and on. **I had no idea that what I was actually dealing with was candida.**

But God knew just who I needed to meet to get headed in the direction to a healthy life. I met Paula over a year ago and we became fast friends. She's like the long lost twin sister I've never met (and anyone who knows more about her knows she actually has a twin, so yeah, I guess that position is already filled. Too bad for me, huh?). Anyway, I started to read her blog posts about candida and thought, hmmm, maybe that's what I've got, but I was too worried about losing weight to worry much about it.

Then after watching me struggle to lose weight for months and months, **Paula asked me to take** Dr. Bakkers' Candida quiz **and I scored well over 200!!** With much love, Paula suggested I get serious about finally kicking my candida to the curb. So, since then I've been starving my candida. It's been quite a journey!

I can't recommend Healing Candida with Food, Paula's first cookbook enough, by the way, it's really made this whole experience so much easier. I've also had a ton of fun playing with many of the recipes here in *The Sweeter Side of Candida*. **They've almost been like medicine to my soul as I've created them with the anticipation that they might help some of you continue in your journey to health.**

So, you may ask, where are you in this journey to beat candida right now?

I still have it. I'm fighting the battle – but don't worry, it'll end with a big knock out! **It's a day-by-day journey to make the right food choices a**nd to do my workouts. You can read more about my love of T-Tapp workouts here.

Today, I'm about 15 lbs. from my healthy goal weight. I'll never be an itty-bitty thing and I'm at the stage in my life where I'm good with that. **I'm learning to embrace the long journey to health and to be focused more on wellness and glorifying God with my eating, than on a number.**

I hope that some of you will join me in my journey! Paula and I started a Facebook group where you can ask both of us questions about beating candida's heiny and get support in your journey.

We're both super busy homeschooling Mamas, so it might take us a bit to get back to you, but we definitely will. **Join our group,** Kicking Candida (with Sarah & Paula).

If you have any questions you'd like to ask me directly, feel free to e-mail me at wholeintentions@gmail.com.

Blessings!

Sarah

PART ONE:

EATING WITH THE ENEMY

Therefore, whether you eat or drink, or whatever you do,

do all to the glory of God.

1 Corinthians 10:31

NEED-TO-KNOW INFO

BAKING TIPS

These recipes were made to our taste - and using our favorite brands. You'll find that Sarah loves lemons, and Paula is light on the sweetener. You might like our recipes just as they are, but perhaps you want them just a tad more sweet or maybe less vanilla-y. Feel free to change them to suit *your* tastes.

As we've created, tweaked, and played, we've learned a lot about baking for a candida diet. Here are our favorite MAKE-NOTE-OF-THESE tips:

1. **There are a LOT of brands of stevia.** Some brands are sweeter than others, some have an aftertaste, some are cheap, some are spendy, and then there's all those off-shoot brands like Truvia (more on that here).

    This makes it hard to follow any cookbook that uses stevia unless you're all using the same brand. Even *we* don't share the same brand! :)

    Everytime we mention stevia in this cookbook, we say to use it 'to taste'. You'll probably want to ring our necks for being so vague, but really, there's no other way around it.

    The best words of advice we can give is to start out *sprinkling* it. Taste test, and sprinkle a little more. Stevia is a LOT sweeter than sugar (like 200-300 times sweeter), so you definitely don't want to use equal proportions, however there is such a thing as too much stevia which can make your baked goods have a bitter aftertaste.

    Play, taste - play, taste. . .

2. **Stevia and salt are best friends.** Some things simply taste better when they're together. So is true with stevia and salt. You'll find that nearly every recipe in here calls for 'a pinch of celtic sea salt' and 'stevia to taste'.

    Stevia and salt have made friendship bracelets, buried a time capsule, and promised to be best friends until the day they die. Do. Not. Separate. ;)

3. **Sometimes xylitol needs to be powdered first.** Xylitol doesn't dissolve as easily as refined white sugar does, so in some recipes it's best to grind it first in a coffee grinder or high-powered blender so it's more like powdered sugar.

Watch the recipes carefully - in some we measure already powdered xylitol, and in others we measure the granules and then powder them. We explain it in detail in the directions.

4. **Stevia and xylitol compliment each other**. Like a good marriage we've found that when a recipe seems like something is missing, it comes together beautifully when both sweeteners are used. Some recipes can stand alone with just one or the other, but others needed them both for that finishing touch (cue violin music).

   There's no right or wrong way to use these two sweeteners, but we found that Paula likes to add stevia first and then top it off with xylitol whereas Sarah likes to start off with xylitol. Each method works well.

   If you want to play around with your own recipes, here is a good Sugar Conversion Chart: http://www.drjacobkeyzernd.com/sweet_calc.htm

5. **Use a bit more sweetener in recipes you're baking or freezing.** When you're using stevia or xylitol in a recipe that you'll be baking or freezing, get it to the point of perfection, and then add just a tad more. When it's almost *too sweet* - it's perfect. Baking and freezing seem to subdue the sweeteners.

6. **Get a spoon, dip your finger, or swipe the beaters**. You have our complete and total permission (like you need it!) to taste your batters, dough, and frostings to tweak the sweetness factor to your liking. Just be sure there's enough to bake with. ;) We both taste all of our batters (a lot!) to make sure that they're just right, so don't be shy, taste away!

7. **A better product results from finer almond flour.** If you're baked goods seem a little grainy and aren't rising very well, make sure you're using a finely ground almond flour. Look for finely ground almond flour or pulse your flour just a bit in a blender, coffee grinder, or food processor. Just be careful - if you blend too much you'll end up with almond butter.

SHOPPING LIST

(This page may contain affiliate links. If you click on those links and buy from that retailer, we earn a commission that does not cost you anything. This helps support our families. Thank you.)

Depending on where you live, many of the ingredients you need won't be available at your local grocery store. Like Sarah, you may have a fantastic health food store near you that carries almost everything, or like Paula, your driveway is permanently engraved with UPS tire tracks. Either way, we've created this list to help you on shopping day.

These particular items are our recommendations. We understand that every family has its own budget (we can't always buy organic either) and preferred brands, so simply do the best you can. We will acknowledge though, that quality products tend to lead to a finer end result.

For an online shopping list visit:

http://wholeintentions.com/shop/sweeter-side-candida-shopping-list/

WHAT YOU'LL NEED:

Items with asterisks (**) are used in several recipes and are "Must Haves" for using this cookbook.

Category	Stages Allowed*	Convenient Baker	Purist Baker
Flours			
Almond Flour **	1, 2, 3	• Just Almonds (use code 'whole' to get 10% off your order) • Honeyville Farms • Bob's Red Mill • Now Foods	Make Your Own Almond Flour (directions at bottom of post)
Coconut Flour **	1, 2, 3	• Tropical Traditions • Nutiva	Make Your Own Coconut Flour

Sweeteners			
Stevia **	1, 2, 3	• Pure NuNaturals Stevia Extract • KAL Pure Stevia • Mountain Rose Herbs	
Xylitol **	1, 2, 3	• Smart Sweet Birch Xylitol	

Oils & Butters			
Coconut Oil **	1, 2, 3	• Tropical Traditions • Wilderness Family Naturals • Nutiva	
Grass Fed Butter **	1, 2b, 3	• We recommend local, grass fed butter	
Raw Almond Butter **	1, 2, 3	• Artisana • Maranatha • Once Again	Make Your Own Nut Butter
Cocoa Butter **	2b, 3	• Mountain Rose Herbs • Raw Organic Indonesian Cocoa Butter	
Coconut Cream/ Coconut Butter/ Coconut Manna	1, 2, 3	• Artisana • Nutiva • Tropical Traditions	Make Your Own Coconut Butter

Milks & Creams			
Almond Milk **	1, 2, 3	• Pacific Naturals Organic	How to Make Almond Milk
Coconut Milk **	1, 2, 3	• Native Forest Organic	How to Make Coconut Milk

Probiotic Dairy			
Greek Yogurt	1, 2b, 3	• Fage	Make Your Own Greek Yogurt
Cream Cheese **	1, 2b, 3	• Green Mountain Farms	

Grains, Beans & Oats

Brown Rice	2, 3	• Bob's Red Mill • Lundberg	
Rolled Oats **	2, 3	• Bob's Red Mill	
Oat Fiber **	2, 3	• NuNaturals • Honeyville Farms	
Black Beans **	2, 3	• Walnut Acres • Eden Foods	Make Your Own Beans
Cannellini Beans	2, 3	• Eden Organic	Make Your Own Beans

Leaveners, Thickeners & Gums

Baking Soda **	1, 2, 3	• Bob's Red Mill • Frontier • Mountain Rose Herbs	
Baking Powder **	1, 2, 3	• Bob's Red Mill • Rumford • Frontier	Homemade Baking Powder
Arrowroot Powder **	2, 3	• Bob's Red Mill • Bulk Herb Store • Mountain Rose Herbs	
Xanthan Gum **	1, 2, 3	• Bob's Red Mill	

Spices & Seasonings

Celtic Sea Salt **	1, 2, 3	• Redmond's Real Salt • Bulk Herb Store	
Ground Cinnamon **	1, 2, 3	• Frontier • Bulk Herb Store • Mountain Rose Herbs	

Ground Nutmeg **	1, 2, 3	• Simply Organic • Mountain Rose Herbs • Frontier	
Ground Ginger **	1, 2, 3	• Frontier • Mountain Rose Herbs • Bulk Herb Store	
Peppercorns	1, 2, 3	• Bulk Herb Store • Mountain Rose Herbs • Spicy World	
Ground Allspice **	1, 2, 3	• Frontier • Mountain Rose Herbs • Simply Organic	
Ground Cloves **	1, 2, 3	• Frontier • Bulk Herb Store • Mountain Rose Herbs	
Cardamom	1, 2, 3	• Frontier • Alpharetta Spice Co. • Mountain Rose Herbs	
Ground Black Pepper	1, 2, 3	• Frontier • Simply Organic • Bulk Herb Store	
Ground Cumin	1, 2, 3	• Frontier • Simply Organic • Bulk Herb Store • Mountain Rose Herbs	
Cayenne	1, 2, 3	• Frontier • Simply Organic • Mountain Rose Herbs • Bulk Herb Store	
Rosemary	1, 2, 3	• Frontier • Bulk Herb Store • Simply Organic • Mountain Rose Herbs	
Vanilla Beans	1, 2, 3	• Frontier • Premium Madagascar Vanilla Beans • Mountain Rose Herbs	

Extracts			
Vanilla **	1, 2, 3	• Batko Flavors • Star Kay White • Mountain Rose Herbs	
Almond **	1, 2, 3	• Star Kay White • Frontier • Simply Organic	
Chocolate	1, 2, 3	• Star Kay White • Frontier • Rodelle Organics	
Peppermint	1, 2, 3	• Star Kay White • Flavorganics • Mountain Rose Herbs	
Nuts & Seeds			
Pecans **	2, 3	• Now Foods • Superior Nut Company	
Macadamias	1, 2, 3	• Bergin Fruit & Nut Company • Superior Nut Company	
Almond Slivers	1, 2, 3	• Just Almonds (use code 'whole' to get 10% off your order) • Mariani	
Walnuts	1, 2, 3	• Good Sense Organic Walnuts • Superior Nut Company	
Almonds	1, 2, 3	• Just Almonds (use code 'whole' to get 10% off your order) • Superior Nut Company	
Sesame Seeds	1, 2, 3	• Bob's Red Mill • Simply Organic	
Chia Seeds **	1, 2, 3	• Garden of Life • Nutiva • Bulk Herb Store	

Flax Meal	1, 2, 3	• Bob's Red Mill • Bulk Herb Store • Garden of Life	
Popcorn	2b, 3	• Arrowhead Mills • Bob's Red Mill • Great Northern Organic	

Teas & Coffees

Pau D'arco Bark	1, 2, 3	• Mountain Rose Herbs • Bulk Herb Store • SunFood • Wisdom Herbs	
Decaffeinated Earl Grey	1, 2b, 3	• Choice Organics • Dalfour	

Decaffeinated Coffee
**
	1, 2b, 3	• Newman's Own
		  Green Mountain
		  Organic K-Cup
		• Marley Coffee Simmer
		  Down	

Fresh Produce & Roots

Ginger Root	1, 2, 3	• Fresh, Local	
Turmeric Root	1, 2, 3	• Fresh, Local	
Green Apples **	2, 3	• Fresh, Local Organic	
Lemons **	1, 2, 3	• Fresh, Local Organic	
Carrots	2, 3	• Fresh, Local Organic	
Blueberries **	2, 3	• Fresh, Local Organic	
Spinach	1, 2, 3	Fresh, Local Organic	
Avocado	2, 3	Fresh, Local Organic	

Pumpkin Puree
**
	2, 3	• Farmer's Market
		  Pumpkin Puree
		  (canned is okay!)
			Fresh, Local Organic (cooked and pureed)

Other			
Eggs **	1, 2b, 3	• Tropical Traditions Fresh, Local Free Range Organic	
Raw Apple Cider Vinegar	1, 2, 3	• Bragg's • Eden's Organics	
Raw Cocoa Powder **	2b, 3	• Navitas • Earth Circle Organics • Mountain Rose Herbs	
Black Strap Molasses	2b, 3	• Wholesome Sweeteners • Plantation	
Alfalfa Leaves	1, 2, 3	• Mountain Rose Herbs • Bulk Herb Store	
Coconut, shredded **	2, 3	• Bob's Red Mill • Tropical Traditions	
Coconut Oil Spray **	1, 2, 3	• Kelapo Coconut Oil Cooking Spray • Spectrum Coconut Oil Spray	

*You'll find a definition of the stages here.

CANDIDA'S LOVE FOR SUGAR

Candida growth is encouraged by several factors:

- antibiotics (drugs, antibiotics found in meat, and chlorinated water - a type of antibiotic)
- a poor immune system
- steroids and other drugs
- a stressful lifestyle
- chemicals and pesticides/herbicides
- diabetes
- mold exposure
- **and . . . the food you eat**

The number one food candida loves is. . .you got it, sugar. Candida hugs it, kisses it, and devours it in one bite. It craves it, dreams about it, and plans exotic vacations with it.

It's just a *tad bit* obsessed.

And candida could care less if it's organic sugar, raw, fruit sugar, honey, white sugar, or corn syrup. Any kind of sugar makes it do the happy dance. And just in case you didn't know - we don't like the candida happy dance.

We can wait while you double-check. . .yep, you're reading a *dessert* cookbook.

Most people have a sweet tooth. We won't lie - we do too! (Guess why we made this cookbook!) Now, we know what you're thinking. **You're asking yourself, "But if candida loves sugar, then aren't we doomed to bread and water for life?"**

NO bread. Just water.

Okay, okay - we aren't serious. No need to cry. :)

While you do need to stay away from the above sugars, you can enjoy the naturally sweet herb stevia and xylitol. These two sweeteners are safe for a candidian to eat. And yes, as of now candidian is a word. Otherwise we'd be known as walking fungus-infested individuals. . . ;)

A WORD ABOUT STEVIA

What is Stevia?

Stevia is a naturally derived sweetener from a stevia rebaudiana shrub originally found in areas of Brazil and Paraguay. The leaves of the shrub are made into an extract that's **200-300 times sweeter than sugar and doesn't raise blood sugar levels because it's calorie free.** High levels of antioxidants have also been found in stevia leaf extracts.

Stevia has been used for over 1,500 years without side effects. In fact, you can grow the plant in your own backyard!

What to Avoid

Unfortunately, as stevia has gained in popularity, there have been off-shoot brands created to fool people into thinking they're buying beneficial stevia, when they're actually only buying a small percentage of stevia mixed with other questionable ingredients. Some of the more popular brands to avoid are Truvia, Nature's Place All Natural Stevia, Stevia In The Raw, Pure Via, and others.

When you're looking for stevia - even organic stevia - be good and cautious of any that contain these 'added' ingredients:

- **erythritol** - a naturally occurring sugar sometimes found in fruit, but unfortunately it's not allowed on a candida diet because it can't be metabolized by oral bacteria, (unlike xylitol). Erythritol is absorbed into the bloodstream after consumption. Naturopath doctor, Dr. Bakker, recommends caution because, "any sugars that stay in the bloodstream too long may feed candida".

- **natural flavors** - is another ingredient that can mean just about anything - whether it's safe or not. If you have concerns, call the company and ask. Some companies really do add natural flavors from plants, and others. . .don't. Double checking is always a good thing.

- **dextrose** – a sweetener that's created from genetically engineered corn.

- **maltodextrin** - a type of sugar that can feed candida and affect your blood sugar levels.

What to Look For in Stevia

1. whole leaf stevia
2. anything that is 100% pure without added ingredients.

Our favorite brands are Pure NuNaturals Stevia Extract*, KAL Pure Stevia, and Mountain Rose Herbs

*NuNaturals Pure Stevia Extract does contain natural flavors. After speaking with the company about the ingredients in their product, we feel we can confidently recommend their pure stevia extract.

sources:
Candida Crusher | Natural News.com | Natural News.com | 100 Days of Real Food

THE XYLITOL CONTROVERSY

//

Disclaimer: Before we begin, let us state that we're not doctors, homeopaths, naturopaths, or scientists. We're simply moms trying to sort out information and share OUR OPINIONS (as of this writing) with you.

****

When it comes to 'alternative' sweeteners, xylitol has been getting a lot of time in the news. **We want to break down the benefits and cautions, as best as we can untangle them, to sort through whether xylitol is a good guy or a bad guy.**

Just What is Xylitol Anyway?

Xylitol is a 5-carbon sugar that can replace sugar in cooking, baking, and as a sweetener for beverages. It's similar in taste and texture to sugar, but has benefits that sugar could only dream of.

Xylitol is a sugar alcohol which means it's not as sweet as sugar, AND it contains 40% fewer calories and 75% fewer carbs. (Doing the happy dance already!)

It is naturally found in fibrous vegetables and fruit - higher amounts are found in plums, raspberries, and cauliflower. **It's also found naturally in us.** It's true - our bodies produce up to 15 grams daily during normal metabolism. Go figure.

Xylitol Concerns

• Because xylitol isn't completely absorbed into your body, **the much-heard-about abdominal gas and diarrhea** can happen. It's not the most pleasant thought though **it seems that it's mainly due to the amount a person eats and what they can tolerate** - and that's going to vary for everyone. Most adults can tolerate at least 40 gm/day while anything over 90 gm/day may have a laxative effect.

　　One holistic doctor noted, *"My experience with clients is that this initial reaction indicates an existing imbalance in the GI tract which is important to be addressed on its own. Once this is cleared, xylitol is well-tolerated and the client is healthier than before."*

　　Our simple words of advice would be to eat xylitol in moderation, just as you would any other food. Since it's used in higher volumes in desserts, let us go ahead and give you this warning now, before you start baking: **desserts *can not* make up an effective candida diet *and should not* make up the bulk of anyone's candida diet.** They should be eaten *occasionally* - not as an everyday occurrence.

　　Enough said.

• We also want to note that **xylitol is toxic to dogs and other pets**. One of the arguments we see a lot is that if xylitol is poisonous/dangerous to pets, why in the world would we eat it ourselves.

Well, just to play good cop, bad cop here - so is chocolate, avocados, macadamia nuts, grapes, raisins, onion, chives, garlic, milk and salt. To us, that argument doesn't hold water - first of all, dogs metabolize foods differently than humans and **you can't convince us that since a dog can potentially die from an avocado or garlic, that we shouldn't eat them. Not gonna happen.**

Just be sure to keep human food out of their four-legged reach. Feed them the kinds of foods they should eat, don't let Fido or Sylvester have access to the counter while you're gone, and they should be fine. ;)

Xylitol Benefits

• **First - and why we're all here, is that it helps fight candida by inhibiting yeast.** Xylitol is alkalinizing (as opposed to sugar which is acidic) to our systems, which makes us less appealing to harmful bacteria, viruses, and fungi. Xylitol and stevia are the only sweeteners that do not feed yeast. It also doesn't cause fermentation so in essence, it's fighting on our side!

• **Xylitol has a glycemic index of 7** (sugar is 60), so there are no highs and lows for your moods and cravings. Xylitol actually helps keep your insulin levels balanced. (This is unlike maltitol, a different sugar alcohol that actually spikes blood sugar.)

• **Non-carcinogenic** - unlike sugar. Need we say more?

• Remember we mentioned that xylitol is a 5-carbon sugar? 5-carbon sugars are antibacterial which is why it's **used in a lot of oral hygiene products like toothpaste, gum, mouthwash, mints, etc.** Some reports claim it inhibits the development of plaque and dental caries.

• **Studies show it decreases ear infections in children.** During World War II in Finland, xylitol was produced from local birch trees. The locals noticed a significant drop in ear infections (and tooth decay). Several studies since then have concluded that xylitol inhibits the growth of Streptococcus pneumoniae and Haemophilus influenzae, both the primary bacteria that causes ear infections.

Conclusion about Xylitol

While fighting candida, natural sugars like local honey aren't an option, though it would be our first choice. We're still a little leery of anything processed however so we do encourage you to use xylitol in *moderation*. A good idea would be to use stevia as much as possible in a recipe, and then add xylitol as needed to get a nice balance of sweetness.

Warning

Unfortunately, as xylitol has become more popular, several brands are being made from corn which is a concern for GMO's among other things. Be sure that when you look for xylitol, you search for the kinds made from birch. One of our favorites is Smart Sweet Birch Xylitol.

sources:

Candida Crusher

Mercola.com

Glycemic Index

Natural News.com

Natural News.com

Fran Sussman.com

aspcs.org

NCBI

NCBI

NCBI

THOUGHTS ON DESSERTS

Before we dig into the recipes, we wanted to chat with you about desserts. . .

We created this book to be an encouragement to you. We know a candida diet isn't always easy so these desserts are our way of giving you a special gift - a long-distance hug while whispering "keep on keeping on".

But while we love our Chocolate Loca Moca Cake and Chocolate Coconut Pecan Bars just as much as the next person, please remember that desserts need to be limited (whether you're on a candida diet or not). As stated previously, **desserts *can not* make up an effective candida diet *and should not* make up the bulk of anyone's candida diet.**

We also want to remind you that xylitol and stevia should be limited. Candida might not be getting 'real sugar' but that doesn't mean you don't have a sweet tooth that wants 'just one more piece' just the same.

The more you eat real, whole foods instead of desserts, the more your body will begin to crave them - and those are the foods that heal.

The title reads *Desserts For the Holidays, Special Occasions, and Everyday Sweet Treats*, but please use wisdom and common sense. If you nourish your body with good food and keep the desserts to a minimum. . .your candida won't stand a chance.

PART TWO:

THE RECIPES

I appeal to you therefore, brothers, by the mercies of God,

to present your bodies as a living sacrifice, holy and

acceptable to God, which is your spiritual worship.

Romans 12:1

COOKIE CRAZE

SNICKER DOODLING COOKIES

(inspired by Katie at Nourishing Simplicity.org)

"These tasty morsels are fantastic with a cup of tea. Sit back, relax, and enjoy a cookie when the afternoon munchies hit." ~ Trisha, Intoxicated On Life

Allowed on:

Stage 1   Stage 2 - *notes below   Stage 3

Ingredients

- 1 stick butter, melted
- 3 Tbs. xylitol granules
- 3/4 c. almond flour
- 1/4 c. coconut flour, packed
- 1/2 tsp. baking soda
- 1/4 tsp. celtic sea salt
- 1 tsp. Earl Grey tea leaves (1 pkg.)
- 1 egg
- 2 Tbs. Earl Grey tea (liquid)
- stevia to taste

Coating:

- 2 Tbs. almond flour
- 1 Tbs. coconut flour
- 1 tsp. cinnamon
- 1/2 tsp. nutmeg
- stevia to taste

Directions

1. Preheat oven to 350 degrees.
2. Make a cup of Earl Gray tea with one tea packet. Set aside to steep.
3. In a small saucepan, melt the butter and xylitol granules together. Stir occasionally until the xylitol has dissolved.
4. In a medium mixing bowl, combine almond flour, coconut flour, baking soda, and celtic sea salt. Rip open one dry Earl Gray tea packet and add the leaves to

the dough.

5. Mix the egg and the butter/xylitol mixture to the dry ingredients and then add 2 Tbs. of Earl Gray tea. Stir well.

6. Add stevia to taste - a little at a time until just a bit too sweet (the sweetness dulls when baking).

7. Let the dough sit for a minute or two to let the coconut flour soak up the liquid while you combine the coating ingredients in a small bowl.

8. With the palms of your hands, roll the dough into balls and then roll them each generously in the coating mixture.

9. Place the balls on a cookie sheet and lightly flatten with the bottom of a glass.

10. Bake for about 15 min. Let cookies sit for 5 minutes on baking sheet, and then cool completely on a wire rack.

*For Stage 2:

• avoid eggs (or try Chia Egg substitute) for the first two weeks.

• be cautious with butter for the first two weeks (or try substituting coconut oil).

AUNT ELLEN'S CHEWY GINGER MOLASSES COOKIES

"This recipe is based on a Ginger Snap recipe that my Great Aunt Ellen hand wrote for me on a recipe card when I wasn't even a teen. Her cookies were so amazing that I had to have the recipe! I'm not even sure I could cook yet! It was fun all these years later, to tweak her famous recipe to share with you." ~ Sarah

Allowed on:

Stage 2 - *notes below   Stage 3

Ingredients

- 4 c. almond flour
- ½ c. oat fiber
- 2 tsp. baking soda
- 1 tsp. celtic sea salt
- 4 tsp. ground ginger
- 2 tsp. cinnamon
- 1 c. xylitol granules
- ½ c. coconut oil, melted and cooled
- 2 eggs
- ½ c. blackstrap molasses
- stevia to taste

Directions

1. Preheat oven to 350 degrees. Line a baking sheet with parchment paper.
2. In a medium bowl combine almond flour, oat fiber, baking soda, celtic sea salt, ground ginger, and cinnamon.
3. In another medium bowl, beat coconut oil, eggs, xylitol, and molasses thoroughly. Mix in dry ingredients.
4. Add stevia to taste - a little at a time until just a bit too sweet (the sweetness dulls when baking).
5. Roll dough into small balls. Place balls on baking sheet at least 3" apart (they will spread quite a bit while baking).
6. Bake for about 10 minutes. Let sit 5-10 minutes on the baking sheet. Cool completely on a wire rack

*For Stage 2:

• avoid eggs (or try Chia Egg substitute) and molasses for the first two weeks.

• be cautious with oat fiber for the first two weeks.

FROSTY THE SUGAR COOKIE

Allowed on:

Stage 2 - *notes below   Stage 3

Ingredients

- 2 c. almond flour, packed
- 1 tsp. baking soda
- 1/2 tsp. celtic sea salt
- 3 Tbs. butter, softened
- 1 Tbs. vanilla extract
- 1/2 tsp. almond extract
- stevia to taste

frosting:

- 4 Tbs. butter
- 4 Tbs. xylitol granules, powdered
- 4 Tbs. arrowroot powder
- 1 tsp. vanilla extract
- 1 tsp. almond extract
- 1 tsp. celtic sea salt
- 1 tsp. almond milk
- stevia to taste

Directions

1. Preheat oven to 325 degrees. Lightly grease baking sheet with butter or coconut oil.

2. In a medium mixing bowl combine almond flour, baking soda, and celtic sea salt. Cut butter into flour mixture with a fork or pastry cutter.

3. Add vanilla and almond extracts and stir with a fork until well combined. The consistency should be crumbly, but hold together nicely if you form it into a ball.

4. Add stevia to taste - a little at a time until just a bit too sweet (the sweetness dulls when baking).

5. Roll the dough out between two sheets of wax or parchment paper to about ¼" thick. Cut cookies with cookie cutters and transfer carefully to baking sheet.

6. Gather up leftover dough pieces and roll out again, cutting more cookies until dough is gone.

7. Bake for 15-20 minutes until lightly browned. Let sit 5-10 minutes on baking sheet and then cool completely on a wire rack before frosting.

8. For the frosting, grind xylitol in coffee grinder or high-powered blender. Combine all ingredients in a small mixing bowl. Add stevia to taste - a little at a time.

*For Stage 2:

• be cautious with butter for the first two weeks (or try substituting coconut oil).

AUNT SARAH'S NO BAKE COOKIES

"I love the easy preparation of this recipe! Scooping and freezing is such a quick process that I immediately made a second batch. I served them to friends who came over for a book study and the consensus among both adults and children was that they were delicious!" ~
Anjanette, *Raising the Barrs*

Allowed on:

Stage 2 - *notes below   Stage 3

Ingredients

- 1/2 c. coconut oil
- 1/4 c. raw cacao powder
- 1 c. almond butter**
- 1/4 tsp. celtic sea salt
- 1 1/2 tsp. vanilla extract
- 1/2 tsp. cinnamon
- 1 1/2 c. quick cooking rolled oats
- 1 c. unsweetened coconut flakes
- 1/2 c. pecans or walnuts
- stevia to taste

Directions

1. In a medium/large saucepan, melt coconut oil and stir in raw cacao powder, almond butter, celtic sea salt, vanilla extract, and cinnamon.

2. Add oats, coconut flakes, and pecans. Add stevia to taste - a little at a time until just a bit too sweet (the sweetness dulls when freezing).

3. Scoop into a mini muffin pan or drop onto a parchment paper lined baking sheet and freeze.

4. Store in the refrigerator or freezer.

*For Stage 2:

• avoid cacao powder for the first two weeks.

• be cautious with oats for the first two weeks.

**you can replace this with an allowed nut butter of choice; but be aware it may change the flavor.

COCONUT PECAN BALLS

Allowed on:

> Stage 2 - *notes below   Stage 3

Ingredients

- 3/4 c. chopped pecans, toasted
- 4 Tbs. xylitol granules
- 1 1/2 c. almond flour
- 1/2 c. unsweetened coconut flakes
- 1/2 tsp. baking soda
- 1/2 tsp. celtic sea salt
- 1 1/2 tsp. cinnamon
- 3/4 tsp. nutmeg
- 3 Tbs. butter, softened
- 1 egg
- 1 1/2 tsp. vanilla extract
- 1 1/2 tsp. almond extract
- stevia to taste

Directions

1. Preheat oven to 350 degrees.
2. Toast pecans on a baking sheet in a single layer for about 10 min. or until just starting to brown. Set aside.
3. In a medium mixing bowl combine all ingredients, adding toasted pecans last.
4. Add stevia to taste - a little at a time until just a bit too sweet (the sweetness dulls when baking).
5. Scoop dough onto lightly greased baking sheet with a medium scoop. Bake for 15-20 minutes. Let cookies sit for 5 minutes on baking sheet, and then cool completely on a wire rack.

*For Stage 2:

• avoid eggs (or try Chia Egg substitute) for the first two weeks.

• be cautious with butter for the first two weeks (or try substituting coconut oil).

CHINESE ALMOND COOKIES

Allowed on:

Stage 2 - *notes below   Stage 3

Ingredients

- 2 c. almond flour
- 1/4 c. oat fiber
- 1/2 tsp. baking soda
- 1/2 tsp. celtic sea salt
- 1/2 c. xylitol granules
- 4 Tbs. butter, cold
- 1 egg, beaten
- 4 tsp. almond extract
- stevia to taste
- blanched almond slivers for topping

Directions

1. Preheat oven to 350 degrees. Line a baking sheet with parchment paper.
2. In a medium bowl combine almond flour, oat fiber, baking soda, salt.
3. Using a fork or a pastry cutter, cut the butter into the dry ingredients until only very tiny bits of butter remain. Add the egg, almond extract, and xylitol and mix well.
4. Add stevia to taste - a little at a time until just a bit too sweet (the sweetness dulls when baking).
5. Roll a small amount of dough between palms of hands to make balls. Place on lined baking sheet about 2" apart.
6. If desired, press cookies flat with the bottom of a glass. Press two almond slivers into each cookie. Let sit 5-10 minutes on the baking sheet. Cool completely on a wire rack.
7. Bake 10-12 minutes, depending on the size of the balls and if you've flattened them. Let cookies sit for 5 minutes on baking sheet, and then cool completely on a wire rack.

*For Stage 2:

- avoid eggs (or try Chia Egg substitute) for the first two weeks.
- be cautious with butter (or try substituting coconut oil) and oat fiber for the first two weeks.

BUTTER ME UP COOKIES

Allowed on:

> Stage 2 - *notes below   Stage 3

Ingredients

- 1/2 c. xylitol granules
- 1/2 c. butter, softened
- 2 pinches of celtic sea salt
- 3 tsp. vanilla extract
- 2 egg yolks
- 2 c. almond flour
- 1/4 c. oat fiber
- 1/4 tsp. baking soda
- stevia to taste

Directions

1. In a medium bowl combine xylitol, butter, celtic sea salt, and vanilla extract and beat until creamy. Beat in the egg yolks.

2. Add the almond flour, oat fiber and baking soda and stir until well incorporated.

3. Add stevia to taste - a little at a time until just a bit too sweet (the sweetness dulls when baking).

4. Knead the dough a few times in the bowl, or on a lightly almond floured board. Place dough on a sheet of plastic wrap, roll it into a log, and wrap tightly. Refrigerate for several hours or overnight.

5. When you're ready to bake, preheat the oven to 350. Line a baking sheet with parchment paper. Slice the refrigerated dough into 1/4 to 1/2 inch rounds. Place about 2" apart on a baking sheet.

6. Bake about 10-12 minutes or until they begin to turn golden brown on the edges. Let cookies sit for 5 minutes on baking sheet, and then cool completely on a wire rack.

*For Stage 2:

• avoid eggs for the first two weeks.

• be cautious with butter (or try substituting coconut oil) and oat fiber for the first two weeks.

DON'T JUDGE ME BY MY LOOKS CHOCOLATE MINT COOKIES

Allowed on:

> Stage 2 - *notes below   Stage 3

Ingredients

- 2 c. almond flour
- 1 tsp. baking powder
- 1/2 c. xylitol granules
- 1/4 c. butter, softened
- 1 tsp. vanilla extract
- 1 tsp. peppermint extract
- 1 Tbs. water
- 1/2 tsp. celtic sea salt
- stevia to taste
- green food coloring (optional)
- 1 c. Homemade Chocolate Chips/ Chunks

Directions

1. Preheat the oven to 350 degrees. Line a baking sheet with parchment paper.
2. In a medium bowl combine all of the ingredients, minus the chocolate chips, until the batter comes together and is nice and smooth.
3. Add stevia to taste - a little at a time until just a bit too sweet (the sweetness dulls when baking).
4. Stir the chocolate chips in by hand until well combined.
5. Form the dough into balls with your hands and place about 3" apart on lined baking sheet. Flatten the cookies with the bottom of the glass (or your hand, if you wish).
6. Bake approximately 15-18 minutes. Let sit 5-10 minutes on the baking sheet. Cool completely on a wire rack.

*For Stage 2:

- avoid cacao powder and cocoa butter (in the Homemade Chocolate Chips/Chunks) for the first two weeks.

- be cautious with butter for the first two weeks (or try substituting coconut oil).

CHEWY CHOCOLATE CHIP COOKIES

Allowed on:

Stage 2 - *notes below   Stage 3

Ingredients

- 2 c. almond flour
- 1/4 c. butter, softened
- 1/2 c. xylitol granules
- 1/2 tsp. celtic sea salt
- 1 tsp. baking powder
- 3 tsp. vanilla extract
- 1/4 tsp. almond extract
- 1 Tbs. decaf coffee
- stevia to taste
- 1/2 recipe of Homemade Chocolate Chips/Chunks, chopped into small pieces

Directions

1. Preheat the oven to 350 degrees. Line a baking sheet with parchment paper.
2. In a medium bowl combine all of the ingredients, minus the chocolate chips, until the batter comes together and is nice and smooth.
3. Add stevia to taste - a little at a time until just a bit too sweet (the sweetness dulls when baking).
4. Stir the chocolate chips in by hand until well combined.
5. Form the dough into balls with your hands and place about 3" apart on lined baking sheet. Flatten the cookies with the bottom of the glass (or your hand, if you wish).
6. Bake approximately 15-17 minutes. Let sit 5-10 minutes on the baking sheet. Cool completely on a wire rack.

*For Stage 2:

• avoid cacao powder and cocoa butter (in the Homemade Chocolate Chips/Chunks) for the first two weeks.

• be cautious with butter for the first two weeks (or try substituting coconut oil).

HARVEST BOUNTY APPLE WALNUT & OATMEAL COOKIES

Allowed on:

Stage 2 - *notes below   Stage 3

Ingredients

- 2 c. almond flour
- 1/2 tsp. baking powder
- 1 tsp. baking soda
- 1 tsp. celtic sea salt
- 3 tsp. cinnamon
- 1/2 tsp. nutmeg
- 3 tsp. vanilla extract
- 3/4 c. butter, softened
- 1/2 c. xylitol granules
- 2 Tbs. fresh lemon juice
- 2 eggs
- 1 c. diced apples, chopped into small chunks
- 1 c. chopped walnuts
- 3 c. quick cooking rolled oats
- stevia to taste

Directions

1. Preheat the oven to 350 degrees.
2. In a medium mixing bowl, combine almond flour, baking powder, baking soda, salt, cinnamon, and nutmeg. Set aside.
3. In another medium mixing bowl, mix vanilla, butter, xylitol, lemon juice and eggs together until creamy.
4. Add the dry mixture to the wet mixture and mix until well combined. Stir the apple, walnuts and rolled oats into the batter with a wooden spoon.
5. If needed, add stevia to taste - a little at a time until just a bit too sweet (the sweetness dulls when baking).
6. Form the dough into balls with your hands and place about 3" apart on lined baking sheet. Flatten the cookies with the bottom of the glass (or your hand, if you wish).
7. Bake approximately 15-17 minutes. Let sit 5-10 minutes on the baking sheet. Cool completely on a wire rack.

*For Stage 2:

• avoid eggs (or try Chia Egg substitute) for the first two weeks.

• be cautious with butter (or try substituting coconut oil) and oats for the first two weeks.

BLONDIES, BROWNIES, AND BARS. . .OH, MY!

LUSCIOUS LEMON-GLAZED BLONDIES

Allowed on:

Stage 1   Stage 2 - *notes below   Stage 3

Ingredients

blondies:

- 1/2 c. xylitol granules
- 1/2 c. butter, softened
- 1/2 c. almond flour
- 1/4 c. coconut flour
- 1/2 tsp. celtic sea salt
- zest of 2 lemons
- 2 eggs, beaten
- 1 Tbs. coconut oil
- juice of two lemons
- stevia to taste

glaze:

- juice from 2 lemons
- zest from 1/2 of a lemon
- 2/3 c. powdered xylitol
- stevia to taste

Directions

1. Preheat oven to 350 degrees. Grease an 8x8 baking dish with coconut oil or butter.

2. Combine xylitol, butter, flours, celtic sea salt, and lemon zest in a medium bowl until nice and creamy. Add beaten eggs, coconut oil, and lemon juice and beat on medium speed until fluffy (about two minutes).

3. Add stevia to taste - a little at a time until just a bit too sweet (the sweetness dulls when baking).

4. Pour batter into baking dish. Bake approximately 25 minutes until edges are brown and blondies are firm. Cool completely.

5. For the glaze, mix lemon juice, zest, xylitol, and stevia in a small bowl until smooth. Pour glaze over blondies and let set for several hours (or even better, overnight).

*For Stage 2:

• avoid eggs (or try Chia Egg substitute) for the first two weeks.

• be cautious with butter for the first two weeks (or try substituting coconut oil).

CHOCOLATE CHUNK FUDGE BROWNIES

Allowed on:

Stage 2 - *notes below   Stage 3

Ingredients

- 1/4 c. xylitol granules
- 1 - 15 oz. can black beans, drained and rinsed well
- 2 eggs
- 1/4 c. raw cacao powder
- 1/2 c. plus 2 Tbs. almond flour
- 1/2 tsp. celtic sea salt
- 1/4 c. butter, softened (1/2 stick)
- 4 tsp. vanilla extract
- 1/2 tsp. baking powder
- stevia to taste
- 1/2 c. Homemade Chocolate Chips/Chunks

Directions

1. Preheat oven to 350. Grease an 8x8 pan with butter or coconut oil.
2. Blend rinsed beans and eggs in blender until there are no bean chunks left. Pour into a medium sized mixing bowl. Add xylitol and all other ingredients, minus the chocolate chips.
3. Add stevia to taste - a little at a time until just a bit too sweet (the sweetness dulls when baking).
4. Add the chocolate chips, stirring well with a spoon.
5. Bake for 15-18 min. until toothpick inserted in middle comes clean. Bake just a tad less if you want a fudgier brownie.
6. Let cool completely before cutting. Serve with Whipped Coconut Cream if desired.

*For Stage 2:

- avoid eggs (or try Chia Egg substitute) for the first two weeks.
- avoid cacao powder and cocoa butter (in the Homemade Chocolate Chips/Chunks) for the first two weeks.
- be cautious with butter for the first two weeks (or try substituting coconut oil).

CHOCOLATE COCONUT PECAN BARS

Allowed on:

Stage 2 - *notes below   Stage 3

Ingredients

crust:

- 1 c. almond flour
- 1/2 c. butter, softened
- 1/2 c. unsweetened shredded coconut
- 1/8 tsp. celtic sea salt
- 1/2 tsp. almond extract
- stevia to taste

filling:

- 1 - 15 oz. can coconut milk
- 1/2 c. xylitol granules
- 1/2 tsp. almond extract
- 4 tsp. vanilla extract
- stevia to taste
- 1/2 recipe of Homemade Chocolate Chips/Chunks, still warm and melted

toppings:

- 1 c. unsweetened shredded coconut
- 1 c. chopped pecans, divided

Directions

1. Preheat oven to 350 degrees. Grease an 8x8 baking dish with coconut oil or butter.

2. Mix all of the crust ingredients together in a small bowl using a pie dough cutter or a fork.

3. Add stevia to taste - a little at a time until just a bit too sweet (the sweetness dulls when baking).

4. Once well mixed, use your hands and form into a nice ball. Put the ball in the baking dish, press down, and spread evenly over the bottom of the dish. Bake approximately 15 minutes, until golden brown. Let cool.

5.   In a medium saucepan over medium/low heat, combine coconut milk, xylitol, and extracts. Add stevia to taste - a little at a time until just a bit too sweet (the sweetness dulls when baking).

6.   Let it simmer until xylitol dissolves and it becomes nice and thick - about 35-40 minutes. Once the mixture is boiling rapidly and has become thick, remove from the heat and pour over the crust.

7.   Prepare half of a recipe of Homemade Chocolate Chips/Chunks. Once it's cooked, let cool a bit and thicken just slightly. Pour over the condensed coconut milk, making sure to cover the entire thing nicely.

8.   Sprinkle 3/4 c. of the chopped pecans over the chocolate layer, then sprinkle the shredded coconut over that, and finish off with the rest of the pecans.

9.   Bake approximately 30 minutes. Cool completely on a wire rack (at least 1 hour) and then refrigerate a couple of hours before cutting and serving.

*For Stage 2:

• avoid cacao powder and cocoa butter (in the Homemade Chocolate Chips/Chunks) for the first two weeks.

• be cautious with butter for the first two weeks (or try substituting coconut oil).

CRUNCHIN' FUDGE BARS

Allowed on:

Stage 2 - *notes below   Stage 3

Ingredients

- 2/3 c. cocoa butter
- 2/3 c. raw cacao powder
- 3 Tbs. xylitol granules
- 1 c. almond butter**
- 1 c. old-fashioned oats
- 1/2 c. unsweetened coconut flakes
- 1/2 c. chopped almonds (or nut of choice)
- 1 tsp. vanilla extract
- stevia to taste
- pinch of celtic sea salt - if almond butter is unsalted

Directions

1. Melt cocoa butter in a medium saucepan over low/medium heat. Add raw cacao powder and xylitol and stir until xylitol is dissolved.
2. Stir in almond butter, oats, coconut flakes, almonds, and vanilla extract.
3. Add stevia to taste - a little at a time.
4. Pour batter in a 9x9 pan greased with butter or coconut oil and refrigerate about 2 hours or until hard. Store in refrigerator.

*For Stage 2:

• avoid cacao powder and cocoa butter for the first two weeks.

• be cautious with oats for the first two weeks.

**you can replace this with an allowed nut butter of choice; but be aware it may change the flavor.

HAVE YOUR CAKE & FROST IT TOO

SPICE DOCTOR MAE'S PUMPKIN CAKE

A special thanks to 'Aunt Mae' who doctored up this cake to make it the deliciousness that it is!

Allowed on:

> Stage 2 - *notes below   Stage 3

Ingredients

- 1 1/2 c. pumpkin puree
- 8 Tbs. butter, softened
- 5 eggs, at room temperature
- 2 tsp. vanilla extract
- 2 1/2 c. almond flour, fine preferred
- 1 1/2 tsp. baking powder
- 1/2 tsp. celtic sea salt
- 1 1/2 tsp. cinnamon
- 1 1/2 tsp. nutmeg
- 1 tsp. ginger
- 1/2 tsp. allspice
- 1/8 tsp. ground cloves
- 1/2 tsp. ground cardamom
- 1/2 c. xylitol granules
- stevia to taste

Directions

1. Preheat oven to 350 degrees. Grease a bundt pan with coconut oil or butter.
2. In a medium mixing bowl beat pumpkin, butter, eggs, and vanilla for about 2 minutes on medium speed. Set aside.
3. Add the dry ingredients to the wet ingredients and continue to mix until well combined.
4. Add stevia to taste - a little at a time until just a bit too sweet (the sweetness dulls when baking).
5. Pour batter into bundt pan and bake for about 45-55 minutes, until a toothpick inserted in the middle comes out clean. Let cake sit about 10 minutes, and then

turn upside down onto plate.

6. Frost with Beater Lickin' Almond Butter Frosting by spooning blobs of the frosting onto the hot cake and letting it melt down the sides. Use extra frosting to serve on top of the cake.

*For Stage 2:

• avoid eggs for the first two weeks.

• be cautious with butter for the first two weeks (or try substituting coconut oil).

NO PLAIN JANE VANILLA CUPCAKES/CAKE

Allowed on:

> Stage 2 - *notes below   Stage 3

Ingredients

- 1 - 15 oz. can Cannellini bean, drained and rinsed well
- 5 eggs
- 5 tsp. vanilla extract
- 1/2 tsp. celtic sea salt
- 1/2 c. coconut oil, melted and cooled
- ⅓ c. xylitol granules
- ¼ c. coconut flour
- 1 tsp. baking powder
- 1/2 tsp. baking soda
- stevia to taste

Directions

1. Preheat oven to 350 degrees. Line a muffin pan with 24 muffin papers or grease 8x8 pan with butter or coconut oil.

2. Blend the beans and eggs in a blender until there are no bean chunks. Pour into a mixing bowl and add the rest of the ingredients, including the xylitol. Mix well.

3. Add stevia to taste - a little at a time until just a bit too sweet (the sweetness dulls when baking).

4. Divide the batter evenly between the cupcake papers or pour into the cake pan and bake for 25 minutes. Let cool.

5. Frost with Beater Lickin' Almond Butter Frosting or Classic & Quick Cream Cheese Frosting.

*For Stage 2:

• avoid eggs for the first two weeks.

CHOCOLATE LOCA MOCHA CAKE

Allowed on:

Stage 2 - *notes below   Stage 3

Ingredients

- 2 - 15 oz. cans black beans, drained and rinsed well
- 10 eggs
- 4 tsp. vanilla extract extract
- 2 tsp. almond extract
- 1 tsp. celtic sea salt
- 2/3 c. coconut oil
- 1/2 c. + 2 Tbs. xylitol granules
- 2/3 c. + 2 Tbs. raw cacao powder
- 2 tsp. baking powder
- 1 tsp. baking soda
- 2 Tbs. decaffeinated coffee
- stevia to taste

Directions

1. Preheat oven to 350 degrees. Line two 9 inch cake pans with parchment paper and grease lightly with butter or coconut oil.

2. Drain beans and rinse. Blend the beans and eggs in a blender until there are no bean chunks. Pour batter into a medium-sized mixing bowl and add the rest of the ingredients, including the xylitol. Mix well.

3. Add stevia to taste - a little at a time until just a bit too sweet (the sweetness dulls when baking).

4. Divide the batter evenly between the two cake pans and bake for 40-45 minutes. Insert a toothpick into the center of one of the cakes to test for doneness. If the toothpick comes out clean, the cake is done. Let cool before turning them out.

5. Frost with Chocolate Loca Mocha Frosting.

*For Stage 2:

• avoid eggs and cacao powder for the first two weeks.

MINI LEMONY TEA CAKES

Allowed on:

Stage 2 - *notes below   Stage 3

Ingredients

cake:

- 8 Tbs. butter, softened
- 4 eggs
- 1/2 tsp. vanilla extract
- 4 Tbs. lemon juice
- 3 tsp. lemon zest
- 1/2 c. xylitol granules
- 2 1/2 c. almond flour
- 1/4 c. oat fiber
- 1 tsp. baking powder
- 1/2 tsp. baking soda
- 1 tsp. celtic sea salt
- stevia to taste

glaze:

- 1/2 c. powdered xylitol
- 1 tsp. lemon zest
- 2 Tbs. lemon juice
- 4 Tbs. butter
- stevia to taste

Directions

1. Preheat oven to 350 degrees. Grease mini pans with coconut oil or butter.

2. In a medium mixing bowl, cream together butter, eggs, vanilla, lemon, lemon zest, and xylitol.

3. Add almond flour, oat fiber, baking powder, baking soda, and salt. Mix until well combined. Add stevia to taste - a little at a time until just a bit too sweet (the sweetness dulls when baking).

4. Spoon the batter into the pans. Bake for 15-25 minutes (depending on the size of your pans) until a toothpick comes out clean.

5. Remove cakes from the oven. Let sit 10-15 minutes before turning out.

6. While cakes are cooling, combine glaze ingredients in a small saucepan and heat until bubbly and beginning to thicken. Remove from heat and let cool and thicken slightly.

7. With a toothpick, poke holes on the tops of the teacakes. Pour the glaze over each of the cake, letting the glaze run down the sides.

Sarah's note:

The longer you let this cake sit, the better it gets. You may want to make it the night before and cool overnight.

*For Stage 2:

• avoid eggs (or try Chia Egg substitute) for the first two weeks.

• be cautious with butter (or try substituting coconut oil) and oat fiber for the first two weeks.

YOU CAN'T CATCH ME, I'M THE GINGERBREAD CAKE (WITH LEMON SAUCE)

Allowed on:

Stage 2 - *notes below   Stage 3

Ingredients

- 1 - 15 oz. can black beans, drained and rinsed well.
- 1 c. molasses
- 4 Tbs. butter, softened
- 4 eggs
- 4 Tbs. xylitol granules
- 1 tsp. baking soda
- 1 Tbs. baking powder
- 1/2 c. coconut flour, packed
- pinch of salt
- stevia to taste

lemon sauce:

- zest from one lemon
- juice from one lemon
- 1/2 c. cold water
- 1 Tbs. arrowroot powder
- stevia to taste

Directions

1. Preheat oven to 325 degrees. Grease bundt pan with coconut oil or butter.

2. Drain and rinse black beans. Pour into a blender and add molasses, butter, eggs, and xylitol. Blend until there are no bean chunks left.

3. Pour batter into medium sized mixing bowl and add baking soda, baking powder, and coconut flour. Blend well. Add stevia to taste - a little at a time until just a bit too sweet (the sweetness dulls when baking).

4. Pour batter into bundt pan and bake for 50 min.

5. Let cool completely before gently loosening from the sides of the pan and flipping onto a plate.

6. For sauce, zest one lemon and sprinkle lemon zest over cake. In a small sauce pan, heat the lemon juice, water, and arrowroot over medium heat until thickened. Whisk smooth.

7. Add stevia to taste - a little at a time until just a bit too sweet (the sweetness dulls

when baking).

8. Pour sauce over cake and serve immediately.

*For Stage 2:

• avoid eggs (or try Chia Egg substitute) and molasses for the first two weeks.
• be cautious with butter for the first two weeks (or try substituting coconut oil).

GRANDMA COLLEEN'S APPLE DAPPLE CAKE

The original recipe is beautifully handwritten on a recipe card that my Grandmother put into a collection of her recipes for me. ~ Sarah

Allowed on:

> Stage 2 - *notes below   Stage 3

Ingredients

- ½ c. butter, softened
- ¾ c. xylitol granules
- 3 eggs
- 2 tsp. vanilla extract
- 2 c. almond flour
- 2 tsp. baking soda
- 1 tsp. baking powder
- ½ tsp. celtic sea salt
- 2 tsp. cinnamon
- ½ tsp. nutmeg
- stevia to taste
- 4 c. chopped green apples, peels on
- 1 c. chopped pecans

Directions

1. Preheat oven to 350. Grease a 9x13 cake pan with coconut oil or butter.

2. In a medium mixing bowl, cream together butter, xylitol, eggs, and vanilla extract. Add the almond flour, baking soda, baking powder, celtic sea salt, cinnamon, nutmeg and mix again until well combined.

3. Add stevia to taste - a little at a time until just a bit too sweet (the sweetness dulls when baking).

4. Add the apple chunks and pecans, stirring by hand until well incorporated.

5. Pour into cake pan and bake approximately 35-40 minutes until cake is firm to the touch. You want it to be just slightly on the underdone side.

6. Let sit several hours before serving for optimal flavor and texture.

*For Stage 2:

- avoid eggs (or try Chia Egg substitute) for the first two weeks.
- be cautious with butter for the first two weeks (or try substituting coconut oil).

"14 CARAT" CARROT CAKE WITH CINNAMON CREAM CHEESE FROSTING

"This is by far the best "bean-cake" recipe I've made. I have several family members on specialized diets and at our family reunion this carrot cake was a hit. Both the cake and frosting are simple to make. It's a new favorite in our house and I'm sure it will be in yours too." ~ Danielle, *More Than Four Walls*

Allowed on:

Stage 2 - *notes below   Stage 3

Ingredients

- 1-15 oz can of Cannellini Beans (white kidney beans), drained and rinsed well
- 5 eggs
- 3 tsp. vanilla extract
- ½ tsp. celtic sea salt
- ½ c. coconut oil, melted and cooled
- 1/3 c. xylitol granules
- 1 tsp. baking powder
- ½ tsp. baking soda
- ¼ c. coconut flour
- 3 tsp. cinnamon
- ½ tsp. nutmeg
- stevia to taste
- 3 c. carrots, shredded
- 1 c. walnuts, chopped

Directions

1. Preheat oven to 350 degrees. Grease a 9x13 pan with butter or coconut oil.

2. Blend the beans and eggs in a blender until there are no bean chunks. Pour into a mixing bowl and add the rest of the ingredients, including the xylitol. Mix well.

3. Add stevia to taste - a little at a time until just a bit too sweet (the sweetness dulls when baking).

4. Pour batter into cake pan and bake 25-30 minutes, until a toothpick inserted into the middle of the pan comes out clean.

5. Let cake sit at least 4 to 6 hours before frosting and serving - any beany flavor will disappear.

6. Frost with Cinnamon Cream Cheese Frosting.

*For Stage 2:

• avoid eggs for the first two weeks.

BEATER LICKIN' ALMOND BUTTER FROSTING

Friendly advice from [Aunt Mae](#), "CAUTION!! DO NOT put fingers into mixer while running to get...just one more taste."

Allowed on:

> [Stage 1](#)   [Stage 2](#) - *notes below   [Stage 3](#)

Ingredients

- 1/2 c. raw almond butter**
- 1/2 stick butter, softened
- pinch of celtic sea salt
- 1/2 tsp. cinnamon
- 1 tsp. vanilla extract
- 1/4 -1/2 c. almond milk - if needed for a nice fluffy consistency
- stevia to taste

Directions

1. Blend all ingredients until smooth. Add stevia to taste - a little at a time.
2. Spread over cakes, cupcakes, cookies, or bars. Place dollops of frosting on a hot cake to create a beautiful glaze.
3. The frosting will harden when refrigerated - bring to room temperature if needed for later use.

*For Stage 2:

• be cautious with butter for the first two weeks.

**you can replace this with an allowed nut butter of choice; but be aware it may change the flavor.

CHOCOLATE ALMOND BUTTER FROSTING

Allowed on:

> Stage 2 - *notes below   Stage 3

Ingredients

- 1 Tbs. xylitol granules, powdered
- 1/2 c. raw almond butter** (if making your own, use unsalted almonds)
- 3 Tbs. raw cacao powder
- 1 tsp. vanilla extract
- 1/2 tsp. almond extract
- almond milk - if needed to thin to desired consistency
- stevia to taste

Directions

1. Grind xylitol in coffee grinder or high-powered blender.
2. Combine all ingredients, except stevia and milk, in a small mixing bowl.
3. Add stevia to taste - a little at a time.
4. The frosting will harden when refrigerated - bring to room temperature if needed for later use.

*For Stage 2:

• avoid cacao powder for the first two weeks.

**you can replace this with an allowed nut butter of choice; but be aware it may change the flavor.

CHOCOLATE LOCA MOCHA FROSTING

Allowed on:

Stage 2 - *notes below   Stage 3

Ingredients

- ½ c. xylitol granules, powdered
- 2 sticks butter
- 10 Tbs. cacao powder
- 1 tsp. vanilla extract
- 1 tsp. almond extract
- 2 Tbs. almond milk
- 2 Tbs. decaffeinated coffee
- stevia to taste

Directions

1. Grind the xylitol in a coffee grinder or high-powered blender.

2. In a small mixing bowl combine all ingredients, including xylitol. Add milk if needed to bring frosting to desired consistency.

3. Add stevia to taste - a little at a time.

4. This makes plenty to cover a two-layered cake.

*For Stage 2:

• avoid cacao powder for the first two weeks.

• be cautious with butter for the first two weeks.

CHOCOLATE CHUNK MOUSSE FROSTING

Allowed on:

<u>Stage 2</u> - *notes below   <u>Stage 3</u>

Ingredients

- 6 eggs
- 3/4 c. coconut oil, softened or melted
- 6 T. butter, softened
- 3 Tbs. raw cacao powder
- 1 1/2 tsp. vanilla extract
- stevia to taste
- <u>Homemade Chocolate Chips/Chunks</u>

Directions

1. Blend eggs, coconut oil, and butter in a blender until smooth and creamy. (It will be a richer yellow if using farm fresh eggs.)

2. Blend in vanilla extract and cacao powder. Add just a bit of stevia at a time to taste.

3. Pour the frosting into a bowl and refrigerate until thickened enough to spread. It can be refrigerated longer, but will need to be brought to room temp be spreadable.

4. Frost and decorate with chunks of <u>Homemade Chocolate Chips/Chunks</u>.

*For Stage 2:

- avoid eggs and cacao powder for the first two weeks.
- be cautious with butter for the first two weeks.

CINNAMON CREAM CHEESE FROSTING

Allowed on:

| Stage 1 | Stage 2 - *notes below | Stage 3 |

Ingredients

- 8 oz. cream cheese, softened (try to find a combo of greek yogurt/cream cheese**)
- 1 stick butter, softened
- 2 Tbs. vanilla extract
- 1/2 tsp. cinnamon
- pinch of celtic sea salt
- stevia to taste

Directions

1. In a small mixing bowl blend all ingredients until smooth.
2. Add stevia to taste - a little at a time.
3. Store in refrigerator. (It will need to be brought to room temp. to be spreadable.)

*For Stage 2:

• no cream cheese allowed for the first two weeks.

• be cautious with butter for the first two weeks.

**if you can't find a product with 'live cultures' the next best option would be to add a probiotic capsule to it and mix in well before using it in the recipe.

CLASSIC & QUICK CREAM CHEESE FROSTING

Allowed on:

> Stage **1**   Stage **2** - *notes below   Stage **3**

Ingredients

- 8 oz. cream cheese, softened (try to find a combo of greek yogurt/cream cheese**)
- 1 stick butter, softened
- 1 tsp. vanilla extract
- 1 tsp. almond extract
- pinch of celtic sea salt
- stevia to taste

Directions

1. In a small mixing bowl blend all ingredients until smooth.
2. Add stevia to taste - a little at a time.
3. Store in refrigerator. (It will need to be brought to room temp. to be spreadable.)

*For Stage 2:

• no cream cheese allowed for the first two weeks.

• be cautious with butter for the first two weeks.

**if you can't find a product with 'live cultures' the next best option would be to add a probiotic capsule to it and mix in well before using it in the recipe.

WHIPPED COCONUT CREAM

Allowed on:

Stage 1   Stage 2 - *notes below   Stage 3

Ingredients

- 1 can full fat coconut milk
- ½-1 tsp. vanilla extract
- stevia to taste
- about 1 Tbs. coconut cream/ coconut butter/coconut manna, optional for desired thickness

Directions

1. Place can of coconut milk in refrigerator overnight.
2. Tip can upside down and open the bottom. Drain out the liquid. (You can save this to put in smoothies.)
3. Scoop out the coconut fat into a small mixing bowl. Using a hand mixer or stick blender, blend until smooth and fluffy. Add just a dash of vanilla extract and stevia to taste.
4. Depending on how thick you'd like it, add about 1 Tbs. of the coconut cream. You can add more or less as desired.
5. Use immediately or store in refrigerator.

WHIPPED COCONUT CREAM CHEESE FROSTING

Allowed on:

Stage **1**   Stage **2** - *notes below   Stage **3**

Ingredients

- 1 can full fat coconut milk
- 8 oz. cream cheese (try to find a combo of greek yogurt/cream cheese**)
- 1 tsp. vanilla extract
- stevia
- about 1 Tbs. coconut cream/ coconut butter/coconut manna

Directions

1. Place can of coconut milk in refrigerator overnight.

2. Tip can upside down and open the bottom. Drain out the liquid. (You can save this to put in smoothies.)

3. Scoop out the coconut fat into a small mixing bowl. Using a hand mixer or stick blender, blend with the cream cheese until smooth and fluffy. Add just a dash of vanilla extract and stevia to taste.

4. Depending on how thick you'd like it, add about 1 Tbs. of the coconut cream. You can add more or less as desired.

5. Use immediately or store in refrigerator.

*For Stage 2:

• no cream cheese allowed for the first two weeks.

**if you can't find a product with 'live cultures' the next best option would be to add a probiotic capsule to it and mix in well before using it in the recipe.

FLUFFY CLOUD FROSTINC

Allowed on:

Stage 1   Stage 2 - *notes below   Stage 3

Ingredients

- ½ c. xylitol granules
- 1/4 c. water
- 2 egg whites
- 1/2 tsp. vanilla
- pinch of sea salt
- stevia to taste

Directions

1. In a small saucepan, combine xylitol and water. Heat until the xylitol is melted and just begins to boil. Remove from heat.

2. In a medium mixing bowl, using a whisk attachment (the mixer should be on medium to medium high speed) whisk egg whites to soft peaks. Mix in vanilla and sea salt until just incorporated.

3. With the mixer on medium speed, very slowly add the xylitol and water mixture in a thin stream. Mix until firm peaks are formed. Taste the frosting and add additional vanilla and stevia (just a little at a time) to taste, if desired.

*For Stage 2:

• avoid eggs for the first two weeks.

ME, OH, MY! PIES & CRUST

TONGUE TINGLING LEMON CHEESECAKE

Allowed on:

Stage **1**   Stage **2** - *notes below   Stage **3**

Ingredients

crust:

- single Just the Basics Almond Pie Crust, prebaked

filling:

- 2 - 8 oz. pkgs. greek yogurt/ cream cheese**
- 3 eggs
- 1 Tbs. lemon juice (a little tart)
- 1 Tbs. vanilla extract
- 1/2 c. xylitol granules

lemon glaze:

- 3-4 Tbs. fresh lemon juice (from 1 lemon)
- 4 Tbs. powdered xylitol
- lemon zest, optional
- lemon slices, for garnish

Directions

1. Preheat oven to 400 degrees and place a stoneware baking sheet (you can also use bricks or an unglazed ceramic tile) in the bottom of the oven. (This helps to hold a steady heat in the oven.)

2. In a small mixing bowl, combine filling ingredients. Pour filling into prebaked pie crust.

3. Right before you put the cheesecake in the oven, turn the heat down to 200 degrees. Bake for about 60 min. or until cake is firm to touch but slightly soft in the center. Remove from oven.

4. You can refrigerate the cake until later or prepare glaze and serve warm.

5. For the glaze: zest a lemon and set the zest aside. Combine lemon juice and xylitol and bring it to a boil - making sure all xylitol is dissolved. Remove from heat and let sit for about 15 min. to cool and thicken. Add the lemon zest to the glaze and pour over individual pieces of cheesecake.

6. You can store the glaze in the refrigerator for later use - it will not harden.

7. Garnish each cheesecake slice with lemon slices.

*For Stage 2:

• cream cheese is not allowed for the first two weeks.

• avoid eggs for the first two weeks.

**if you can't find a product with 'live cultures' the next best option would be to add a probiotic capsule to it and mix in well before using it in the recipe.

COCONUT CUSTARD PIE

Allowed on:

Stage 2 - *notes below   Stage 3

Ingredients

- 1 c. shredded coconut
- 5 eggs
- 1 c. coconut cream/ coconut butter/coconut manna
- 1 c. almond milk
- 2 tsp. vanilla extract
- 3/4 c. almond flour
- 1/2 c. butter, softened
- 1/2 c. xylitol granules
- 1/2 tsp. baking powder
- 1/2 tsp. celtic sea salt
- stevia to taste
- cinnamon for sprinkling

Directions

1. Preheat oven to 350. Grease a pie plate with coconut oil or butter.
2. Blend all the ingredients except stevia and cinnamon in a blender.
3. Add stevia to taste - a little at a time until just a bit too sweet (the sweetness dulls when baking).
4. Pour batter into pie plate.
5. Bake about 45 minutes until set and toothpick comes out clean.
6. Sprinkle top with cinnamon. Cool and refrigerate at least 3 hours before serving.

*For Stage 2:

• avoid eggs for the first two weeks.
• be cautious with butter for the first two weeks (or try substituting with coconut oil).

TWICE THE SPICE PUMPKIN PIE

Allowed on:

Stage 2 - *notes below   Stage 3

Ingredients

crust:

- single It's a Gingersnap Pie Crust, unbaked

filling:

- 1 c. coconut milk (1 CUP, not 1 can)
- 1 - 15 oz. can pumpkin puree
- 3 eggs
- 1/2 c. + 1 Tbs. xylitol granules
- 2 tsp. vanilla extract
- 2 tsp. cinnamon
- 1 tsp. ginger
- 1 tsp. cloves
- 1 tsp. allspice
- 1 tsp. celtic sea salt

Directions

1. Place can of coconut milk in refrigerator overnight.
2. The next day, preheat the oven to 350.
3. Tip the coconut milk can upside down and open the bottom. Drain out the liquid. (You can save this to put in smoothies.)
4. Scoop the coconut fat into a medium mixing bowl and let soften a bit. Using a hand mixer or stick blender, blend with the pumpkin, eggs, xylitol, vanilla, and all the spices.
5. Add stevia to taste - a little at a time until just a bit too sweet (the sweetness dulls when baking).
6. Pour into unbaked pie crust.
7. Bake at 350 for 50-60 min. or until a knife inserted in the middle comes out clean.

8. Serve warm with Whipped Coconut Cream or refrigerate until later. Store leftover slices in refrigerator.

Paula's notes:

This version is a bit spicier than normal. You can easily swap out a different pie crust, and tone down the filling by using half the amount of vanilla extract, cinnamon, ginger, cloves, and allspice. Taste a little of the filling and decide if you want to add more.

*For Stage 2:

• avoid eggs (or try Chia Egg substitute) for the first two weeks.

YOU'RE THE APPLE OF MY PIE

Allowed on:

Stage 2 - *notes below   Stage 3

Ingredients

crust:

- Two Just the Basics Almond Pie Crust, unbaked

filling:

- 6 Granny Smith apples, cored, peeled and sliced into 1/2 inch thick slices
- 1 Tbs. lemon juice
- 1 Tbs. arrowroot powder
- 1/2 tsp. cinnamon
- 1/4 tsp. nutmeg
- 1 Tbs. butter, cut into pieces
- stevia to taste

Directions

1. Preheat oven to 450 degrees.
2. Divide the pie crust dough in half. Press one of the halves into a pie plate. Roll out the other half between two sheets of wax paper. Remove top piece of wax paper. Set pie crust aside.
3. In a medium mixing bowl, combine apples, lemon juice, arrowroot powder, cinnamon, and nutmeg.
4. Add stevia to taste - a little at a time until just a bit too sweet (the sweetness dulls when baking).
5. Pour filling into unbaked pie crust. Cut up the butter into pieces and lay randomly over filling.
6. Carefully lay the rolled out pie crust on top of the filling and gently peel back the wax paper. Seal edges and flute. Place pie cover over edges or cover edges with foil to prevent burning. Lightly lay a sheet of foil overtop the pie crust.
7. Bake for 15 minutes. Reduce heat to 350, remove sheet of foil, and bake 45 min. longer.
8. Serve warm with Whipped Coconut Cream or refrigerate until later. Store leftover slices in refrigerator.

*For Stage 2:

- be cautious with butter for the first two weeks or omit.

PEEKIN' PECAN PIE

Allowed on:

Stage 2 - *notes below   Stage 3

Ingredients

crust:

- single Just the Basics Almond Pie Crust, unbaked

filling:

- 8 Tbs. butter
- 1/4 c. + 2 T. xylitol granules
- 2 eggs
- 1 ½ tsp. arrowroot powder
- 1 Tbs. almond or coconut milk
- pinch of celtic sea salt
- 2 tsp. cinnamon
- 1 tsp. vanilla extract
- stevia to taste
- 1 1/2 c. pecans, divided

Directions

1. Preheat oven to 350 degrees.
2. Toast 1 c. of chopped pecans by laying them in a single layer on a baking sheet and baking for about 10 minutes or until just starting to brown. Set aside.
3. Melt butter and xylitol until xylitol is dissolved. Let it cool enough so that it won't cook the eggs when you're adding the rest of the ingredients.
4. Combine melted butter/xylitol with the rest of the ingredients.
5. Add stevia to taste - a little at a time until just a bit too sweet (the sweetness dulls when baking).
6. Sprinkle toasted pecans onto the crust. Pour the filling over the pecans.
7. Sprinkle the other 1/2 c. of un-toasted pecans on top. They will rise to the top during baking.
8. Place pie cover on pie to protect edges from burning or put foil around the edge.
9. Bake for 15 minutes. Turn heat down to 300 and bake for 45-55 minutes or until done.

*For Stage 2:

• avoid eggs (or try Chia Egg substitute) for the first two weeks.

• be cautious with butter for the first two weeks.

I'M SO BLUEBERRY PIE

Allowed on:

Stage 2 - *notes below   Stage 3

Ingredients

crust:

* two Just the Basics Almond Pie Crust, unbaked

filling:

* 5 c. fresh blueberries OR 8 c. frozen blueberries, thawed and drained well
* 1 Tbs. lemon juice
* 3 Tbs. arrowroot powder
* 1/2 tsp. cinnamon
* pinch of celtic sea salt
* stevia to taste

Directions

1. Preheat oven to 400 degrees.
2. In a medium mixing bowl, sprinkle blueberries with lemon juice and let sit to the side.
3. Divide the pie crust dough in half. Press one of the halves into a pie plate. Roll out the other half between two sheets of wax paper. Remove top piece of wax paper. Set pie crust aside.
4. Add arrowroot powder, cinnamon, and celtic sea salt to blueberries and mix gently. Add stevia to taste - a little at a time until just a bit too sweet (the sweetness dulls when baking).
5. Pour filling into unbaked pie shell.
6. Take the other crust gently place on top of the pie. Carefully peel back the wax paper then seal and flute edges.
7. Cover edges of pie with pie cover or foil to prevent over browning.
8. Bake for 35 minutes. If you notice the top getting too brown, lay a sheet of aluminum foil over top.

DOUBLE TROUBLE LAYERED PUMPKIN CHEESECAKE

Allowed on:

Stage 2 - *notes below   Stage 3

Ingredients

crust:

- 2 c. almond flour, packed
- 1 tsp. baking soda
- 1/2 tsp. celtic sea salt
- 1/2 tsp. almond extract
- 1 T. vanilla extract
- 5 Tbs. butter, softened
- stevia to taste

1st layer:

- 1 recipe Whipped Coconut Cream Cheese Frosting, divided

2nd layer:

- 1 - 15 oz. can pumpkin puree
- 8 oz. cream cheese (look for greek yogurt/cream cheese**)
- 3 eggs
- 1 stick butter, softened
- 1/4 c. almond flour
- 1 tsp. vanilla extract
- 1 tsp. cinnamon
- 1 tsp. nutmeg
- stevia to taste

Directions

1. Preheat the oven to 350 degrees and grease a springform pan with butter or coconut oil.

2. Mix the crust in a small mixing bowl, combining almond flour, baking soda, salt, and almond and vanilla extracts.

3. Cut in the butter with a pastry cutter and add stevia to taste - a little at a time until just a bit too sweet (the sweetness dulls when baking). Press crust into bottom of the springform pan.

4. For the 1st layer, take the Whipped Coconut Cream Cheese Frosting and divide evenly - setting one half to the side (for serving). Carefully spread the other half on top of the crust.

5. For the 2nd layer, cream together the pumpkin, cream cheese, eggs, and butter. Whisk in the rest of the ingredients, adding stevia to taste - a little at a time. Mix well and pour over the cream cheese layer.

6. Bake for about 45 minutes. Make sure not to over bake - the center should be just a little jiggly. Cool completely. You can refrigerate until ready to serve.

7. Remove sides of springform pan before serving. Serve with a dollop from the other half of the Whipped Coconut Cream Cheese Frosting.

8. Store in the refrigerator.

*For Stage 2:

• cream cheese is not allowed for the first two weeks.

• avoid eggs (or try Chia Egg substitute) for the first two weeks.

• be cautious with butter for the first two weeks.

**if you can't find a product with 'live cultures' the next best option would be to add a probiotic capsule to it and mix in well before using it in the recipe.

LICK YOUR LIPS LEMON MERINGUE PIE

Allowed on:

Stage 2 - *notes below   Stage 3

Ingredients

crust:

- 1 1/4 - 1 1/2 c. almond flour (enough to make the pie crust stay together)
- 1/2 c. butter, melted
- stevia to taste
- pinch of celtic sea salt

pie filling:

- 3 egg yolks, beaten
- 3/4 c. xylitol granules
- 1/4 c. arrowroot
- 1/4 tsp. celtic sea salt
- 1 c. water
- 3 Tbs. butter
- 1/3 c. lemon juice (you can go up to 1/2 c if you like your pie tart)
- 1 1/2 Tbs. lemon zest (you can go up to 2 T if you like your pie tart)
- stevia to taste

meringue:

- 3 egg whites (If you like a really fluffy meringue topping, you may want to double the egg whites)
- stevia to taste
- 1/4 tsp. arrowroot

Directions

1. Preheat oven to 400 degrees for crust. Grease a pie plate with coconut oil or butter.
2. In a small bowl, mix almond flour, butter, and salt together for crust. Add stevia to taste - a little at a time until just a bit too sweet (the sweetness dulls when baking).

3. Pat crust into pie plate so that it covers the bottom and goes up the sides. Bake about 10 minutes, until golden brown. Cool completely.

4. Beat 3 egg yolks and set aside. In a medium saucepan, over medium heat, combine xylitol, arrowroot, celtic sea salt and water - stirring constantly. Boil for 1 minute (it will get very thick; this is normal).

5. In very tiny amounts, slowly stir half of the hot mixture into the beaten egg yolks. Then add the egg yolk mixture back to the saucepan. Bring to a boil again and boil for another minute.

6. Stir in butter, lemon juice, lemon zest and stevia - just a little at a time. Remove from heat and pour into the baked pie shell. Let cool.

7. Beat 3 egg whites on medium speed until they turn white. Add arrowroot and stevia to taste and beat until stiff peaks form. Spoon the meringue over the lemon filling; making sure to seal the edges with the meringue.

8. Bake pie for 8 to 10 minutes until meringue is beautifully golden.

9. Refrigerate for several hours before serving. Store in refrigerator.

*For Stage 2:

• avoid eggs for the first two weeks.

• be cautious with butter for the first two weeks (or try substituting coconut oil).

JUST THE BASICS ALMOND PIE CRUST

(makes 1 single crust)

Allowed on:

Stage 1   Stage 2 - *notes below   Stage 3

Ingredients

- 1 1/2 c. almond flour
- 4 Tbs. cold butter OR cold coconut oil
- stevia to taste
- pinch of salt

Directions

1. In a small mixing bowl, combine ingredients with a fork or pastry cutter and press into a pie plate.
2. For a prebaked crust, bake at 375 degrees for 8-10 minutes. Let cool slightly before filling.

*For Stage 2:

• be cautious with butter for the first two weeks.

IT'S A GINGERSNAP PIE CRUST

(makes 1 single crust)

Allowed on:

Stage 1   Stage 2 - *notes below   Stage 3

Ingredients

- 1 1/2 c. almond flour
- 4 Tbs. cold butter OR cold coconut oil
- 1 1/2 tsp. ginger
- 1/2 tsp. cinnamon
- stevia to taste
- pinch of salt

Directions

1. In a small mixing bowl, combine ingredients with a fork or pastry cutter and press into a pie plate.
2. For a prebaked crust, bake at 375 degrees for 8-10 minutes. Let cool slightly before filling.

*For Stage 2:

• be cautious with butter for the first two weeks.

DELIGHTFULLY DECADENT DESSERTS (A.K.A. RANDOM GOODNESS)

ROYAL RICE PUDDING

Allowed on:

Stage 2 - *notes below   Stage 3

Ingredients

- 1 c. brown rice
- 2 c. almond or coconut milk
- 4 Tbs. xylitol granules
- pinch of celtic sea salt
- stevia to taste
- 1 tsp. vanilla extract
- 1/4 tsp. cinnamon

Soaked Rice Directions

1. Soak brown rice in 4 cups of water for about 16-24 hours.

2. Drain water and rinse rice.

3. In a medium saucepan, over medium heat, combine rice, almond or coconut milk, xylitol, salt, and stevia - just a little at a time.

4. Bring to a boil.

5. Turn stove top to low and let simmer for about 30 min. or until rice is tender. Stir often and add more milk if needed to keep it nice and creamy.

6. Add vanilla and remove from heat. Sprinkle with cinnamon before serving warm or refrigerate and serve cold. Store in refrigerator.

Unsoaked Directions

1. In a medium saucepan, over medium heat, combine rice, almond or coconut milk, xylitol, salt, and stevia - just a little at a time.

2. Bring to a boil.

3. Turn stove top to low and let simmer for about 45-60 min. or until rice is tender. Stir often and add more milk if needed to keep it nice and creamy.

4. Add vanilla and remove from heat. Sprinkle with cinnamon before serving warm or refrigerate and serve cold. Store in refrigerator.

FINGER-LICKING CINNAMON ROLLS

"'These are amazing!' my husband declared upon his first bite of these cinnamon rolls. These cinnamon rolls are perfect for a Saturday morning brunch or a healthy sweet treat for the kids after school! They're sure to make your whole family happy." Trisha, Intoxicated on Life

Allowed on:

Stage 1 - *notes below   Stage 2 - *notes below   Stage 3

Ingredients

- ½ c. + 1 Tbs. xylitol granules
- 4 1/2 c. almond flour
- 3/4 tsp. baking soda
- 3/4 tsp. celtic sea salt
- 9 Tbs. softened butter or coconut oil
- 3 eggs
- stevia to taste

filling:

- 6 Tbs. cinnamon
- 6 Tbs. butter, softened

syrup:

- 9 Tbs. cold water
- 1 Tbs. arrowroot powder, optional
- 9 Tbs. butter, softened
- 1 1/2 tsp. vanilla extract
- 1 1/2 Tbs. cinnamon
- stevia to taste

topping:

- 1 1/2 c. pecans (or walnuts), toasted

frosting:

- 8 oz. cream cheese, softened
- 1/2 c. butter, softened (one stick)
- 1 tsp. vanilla extract
- 1 tsp. almond extract
- pinch of celtic sea salt
- stevia to taste

Directions

1. In a medium bowl, combine xylitol with almond flour, baking soda, celtic sea salt, butter or coconut oil, eggs, and stevia. (Add stevia to taste - a little at a time until just a bit too sweet (the sweetness dulls when baking).

2. ⁓ the dough onto wax or parchment paper. Place another sheet of paper on ⁓ roll out to a rectangle about 12x16. Place flat in the refrigerator for about

   ⁓h is in the fridge, cream the filling ingredients together with a fork in ⁓. Set aside.

   ⁓ve dough from fridge and peel off top layer of wax paper. Spread the filling evenly over the dough and begin to roll the dough into a log. (I find it's easiest to pick up one side of the bottom wax paper and gently lift while folding the dough back with a butter knife to get it started. Continue to use the knife and wax paper to help you roll it.

5. Once the log is rolled to one end of the wax paper, wrap the log up in the wax paper and place in the freezer until its hardened. About 2 hours.

6. While the dough is in the freezer, make the syrup. First whisk the cold water and arrowroot together with a fork. Pour it into a small saucepan and add the other ingredients. Bring to a boil and then remove from heat and let cool. While it cools it will thicken. Set aside.

7. Preheat the oven to 350 degrees. Spread the pecans on a baking sheet in a single layer and bake for about 10 minutes or until they start to brown just slightly. Let cool.

8. Grease a 9x13 pan lightly with butter or coconut oil. Cut the frozen dough log into about 2 inch slices. Arrange each roll into the pan with the cut side up.

9. Bake for about 20 min. until just lightly browned. Place a piece of tinfoil, with the shiny side up, on top of the rolls and bake for another 10 min. or so until an inserted toothpick just comes clean. Let cool slightly.

10. Spread the syrup over the rolls and sprinkle with the toasted pecans.

11. Combine the frosting ingredients in a small mixing bowl until smooth and creamy. Add the stevia just a little at a time until sweetened to your liking. When the rolls are cooled, spread or pipe it over the top.

12. Store in refrigerator with snug fitting lid - they tend to dry out otherwise.

*For Stage 1:

• Arrowroot is not allowed. Omit for this stage.

*For Stage 2:

• avoid eggs (or try Chia Egg substitute) for the first two weeks.
• be cautious with butter for the first two weeks - you can try substituting coconut oil in the rolls, but it may not sub well in the frosting.

BAKE EM' BLUEBERRY COBBLER

Allowed on:

| Stage 2 - *notes below | Stage 3 |

Ingredients

- 4 c. of fresh blueberries (enough to nicely cover an 8x8 pan)
- stevia to taste

wet:

- 3 eggs, beaten
- 1 c. coconut milk, stirred (1 CUP, not 1 can)
- 1 tsp. vanilla extract
- 1 Tbs. butter, softened

dry:

- 1/2 c. almond flour
- 1/2 c. coconut flour, packed
- 1/2 tsp. baking soda
- 1/2 tsp. celtic sea salt
- 1/2 tsp. cinnamon
- 1/2-1 tsp. lemon zest
- stevia to taste

topping: (optional)

- coconut milk
- stevia

Directions

1. Preheat oven to 350. Grease an 8x8 baking pan with coconut oil or butter.
2. Pour berries into the baking pan. Sprinkle with stevia to taste - a little at a time until just a bit too sweet (the sweetness dulls when baking).
3. Pour all of the wet ingredients in a medium size bowl and beat well. Add the dry ingredients and beat again until well mixed.
4. Pour the batter over the berries and spread evenly over the top. Bake approximately 45 minutes until top is nicely set and browning.
5. Once the cobbler is done, for an additional treat, stir whatever coconut milk is left from the can with a shake or two of stevia and pour a little over the cobbler.

*For Stage 2:

• avoid eggs (or try Chia Egg substitute) for the first two weeks.

• be cautious with butter for the first two weeks (or try substituting coconut oil).

APPLE CRISP YUMMINESS

Allowed on:

> Stage 2 - *notes below   Stage 3

Ingredients

filling:

- 6 green apples, thinly sliced (no need to peel, but you may if you prefer)
- 4 Tbs. butter
- 1 Tbs. xylitol granules
- ½ tsp. vanilla extract
- ½ tsp. cinnamon
- ¼ tsp. celtic sea salt
- stevia to taste

topping:

- 1 ½ c. quick cooking rolled oats
- 1 c. almond flour
- ¼ tsp. celtic sea salt
- ½ tsp. xanthan gum
- 1 tsp. cinnamon
- ¼ tsp. nutmeg
- ½ c. butter, softened
- stevia to taste

Directions

1. Preheat oven to 350 degrees. Grease an 8x8 baking dish with coconut oil or butter. Arrange apple slices evenly in the baking dish.
2. Melt the butter for the filling and stir in the xylitol, vanilla extract, cinnamon, salt, and stevia - adding a little at a time until just a bit too sweet (the sweetness dulls when baking).
3. Pour the filling mixture over the apples and stir everything together gently until the apples are nicely coated.
4. In a medium size bowl, stir together oatmeal, almond flour, salt, xanthan gum, cinnamon, and nutmeg. Add the softened butter and then a little bit stevia at a time until just a bit too sweet (the sweetness dulls when baking).
5. Mix together until everything forms into a ball. With your hands, crumble bits of the ball over the filling until it's coated evenly.
6. Bake 45 minutes or until nicely browned and the apples are soft.

*For Stage 2:

- be cautious with butter (or try substituting coconut oil) and oats for the first two weeks.

PUMPKIFIED CHEESECAKE MOUSSE

"I really liked the pumpkin cheesecake mousse. It was very creamy and had a nice pumpkin flavor. I was almost expecting it to have a greasy feel to it with the butter in it, but it didn't. My family really enjoyed it!" Jennifer, *Owen Family Six*

Allowed on:

Stage **2** - *notes below   Stage **3**

Ingredients

- 2 T. chia seeds
- 1/2 c. + 1 Tbs. xylitol granules, powdered
- 1 - 15 oz. can pumpkin puree
- 1 tsp. cinnamon
- 1/2 tsp. ginger
- 1/4 tsp. cloves
- 1/2 c. + 1 Tbs. almond or coconut milk
- 8 oz. cream cheese, softened
- 1 stick butter, softened
- 2 tsp. vanilla extract
- 1 tsp. almond extract
- pinch of celtic sea salt
- stevia to taste
- pecans

Directions

1. Grind chia seeds and xylitol in small coffee grinder or high powered blender until a very fine powder.
2. In a medium mixing bowl, combine ground chia seeds and xylitol with all the other ingredients except the stevia and pecans. Blend well. Add stevia to taste - a little at a time.
3. Refrigerate about 1 hour before serving. Garnish with pecans before serving.
4. Store in refrigerator.

*For Stage 2:

- cream cheese is not allowed for the first two weeks.
- be cautious with butter for the first two weeks.

CHOCOLATE CHUNK MOUSSE

Allowed on:

Stage 2 - *notes below   Stage 3

Ingredients

- 6 eggs
- 3/4 c. coconut oil, softened or melted
- 6 T. butter, softened
- 3 Tbs. raw cacao powder
- 1 1/2 tsp. vanilla extract
- pinch of celtic sea salt
- stevia to taste
- ½ c. Homemade Chocolate Chips/Chunks

Directions

1. Blend eggs, coconut oil, and butter in a blender until smooth and creamy. (It will be a richer yellow if using farm fresh eggs.)
2. Blend in cacao powder, vanilla extract, and salt. Add stevia to taste - a little at a time. Stir in chocolate chips by hand.
3. Spoon mousse into a small serving bowl and refrigerate about 1 hour or until thickened to desired consistency.

Paula's note:

Add a few drops of mint extract to make it Chocolate Mint Mousse!

*For Stage 2:

- avoid eggs and cacao powder for the first two weeks.
- be cautious with butter for the first two weeks.

SERIOUS CHOCOLATE LOVERS POT DE CREME

Allowed on:

Stage 2 - *notes below   Stage 3

Ingredients

- 3/4 c. coconut cream/ coconut butter/ coconut manna
- 1/4 c. coconut milk
- 1 c. almond milk
- 6 egg yolks
- 2 pinches of celtic sea salt
- 1/2 tsp. almond extract
- 1/2 tsp. vanilla extract
- 1/4 c. raw cacao powder
- 2 Tbs. decaffeinated coffee, cooled
- stevia to taste

Directions

1. Preheat oven to 300 degrees. If you're using a solid coconut cream, run it under hot water until it's soft.

2. Put all ingredients in your blender and blend really well. Add stevia last - a little at a time until just a bit too sweet (the sweetness dulls when baking).

3. Pour mixture into 3 ramekins.

4. Place ramekins in a large roasting pan. Pour hot water in the roasting pan until it is above 1/2 way up the ramekins. Cover the roasting pan tightly with aluminum foil.

5. Pierce the foil in several places to release the steam. Bake approximately 40-50 minutes.

6. You want the pots to still be jiggly in the center. Remove from pan from the oven and the ramekins from the roasting pan. Place on a wire rack for 1 hour.

7. Once cooled, refrigerate for at least 3 hours before serving. Store in refrigerator.

*For Stage 2:

• avoid eggs and cacao powder for the first two weeks.

notes:

Save your egg whites for Fluffy Cloud Frosting.

FEET IN THE SAND COCONUT ICE CREAM

Allowed on:

> Stage 2 - *notes below   Stage 3

Ingredients

- 2 cans coconut milk
- 1 vanilla bean, scraped or 1-2 tsp. vanilla extract
- 1/2 c. coconut, shredded
- 2 pinches celtic sea salt
- stevia to taste

Directions

1. Pour coconut milk into a large bowl (be sure to scrape all of the cream into the bowl as well).

2. Add the vanilla bean/extract, shredded coconut, and sea salt.

3. Using a hand mixer, mix until well combined. Add stevia to taste (add stevia until just very slightly too sweet—it'll get less sweet after freezing) and any add-ins that you might enjoy and mix again.

4. Pour the mix into an ice cream machine or a 9x13 parchment lined pan and freeze until solid.

5. Scoop into a bowl when ready to eat.

Ice Cream photographed with Chocolate Chunk/Chips added in.

Sarah's note:

Get creative and make your favorite flavors: blueberry, lemon, chocolate, macadamia and chocolate, almond butter and chocolate, peppermint, etc. Have fun with it!

SESAME TOFFEE CANDY

Allowed on:

Stage 1   Stage 2 - *notes below   Stage 3

Ingredients

- 3/4 c. sesame seeds
- 1 c. butter
- 1 c. xylitol granules
- 1/2 tsp. celtic sea salt
- 1/2 tsp. xanthan gum
- 1/2 tsp. baking soda

Directions

1. Toast sesame seeds in a 350 degree oven for just a few minutes until golden (watch them carefully). Set aside.

2. Line a baking sheet with parchment paper and grease it with coconut oil or butter.

3. In a big pot with a candy thermometer, melt butter over medium heat. Stir in xylitol, salt, and xanthan gum. Stir constantly until the candy thermometer reaches 300 degrees (or hard crack stage).

4. Stir in toasted sesame seeds. Remove from heat and stir in baking soda. It will fizzle; this is normal.

5. Pour mixture onto the baking sheet and spread as thinly as possible. Let sit about 30 minutes and then freeze until hard. Store in freezer.

*For Stage 2:

• be cautious with butter for the first two weeks.

SMASHING ENGLISH TOFFEE

"These treats were such a hit with my kids that the morning after I made them, I was met in the kitchen by all three of them (including the 18 month old) chanting, 'Toffee! Toffee! Toffee!' They had to wait until after lunch, which according to them, was practically impossible." ~ Sarah

Allowed on:

Stage **2** - *notes below   Stage **3**

Ingredients

toffee:

- 3 c. almonds
- 2 c. butter
- 2 c. xylitol granules
- 1/4 tsp. celtic sea salt
- 2 tsp. vanilla extract
- 1/2 tsp. xanthan gum

chocolate coating:

- 1 c. coconut oil
- 1/2 c. raw cacao powder
- 2 pinches celtic sea salt
- stevia to taste

optional chocolate coating:

- Homemade Chocolate Chips/Chunks, still warm and melted

Directions

1. Preheat oven 350 degrees. Cover a baking sheet with parchment paper and grease it with coconut oil or butter.

2. On another baking sheet, spread almonds evenly and bake about 10 minutes. Slide the almonds on the sprayed/greased baking sheet and spread out evenly.

3. In a large pot, with a candy thermometer, melt butter over medium heat. Stir in xylitol, salt, vanilla extract, and xanthan gum. Stir constantly until the thermometer reaches 300 degrees (hard crack stage).

4. Pour evenly over the almonds on the baking sheet. Let sit for awhile and prepare chocolate topping.

5. Melt coconut oil and stir in raw cacao powder, celtic sea salt and stevia - just a

little at a time. Once it's all incorporated, remove from the heat and pour evenly over the toffee. Put the baking sheet in the freezer until the candy is set.

6. Once it's hard and chilled, crack it into small pieces. Store in the freezer.

*For Stage 2:

• avoid cacao powder for the first two weeks.
• be cautious with butter for the first two weeks.

ALMOND BUTTER FUDGE

Allowed on:

Stage 1   Stage 2 - *notes below   Stage 3

Ingredients

- 1/2 c. butter
- 2 c. xylitol granules
- 1/4 c. almond milk
- 1/4 c. coconut milk
- 2 pinches of celtic sea salt
- 1/2 tsp. xanthan gum
- 1 c. raw almond butter**
- 1 tsp. vanilla extract
- 1/2 tsp. almond extract
- 1 c. xylitol, powdered
- stevia to taste

Directions

1. Melt butter in a medium pot over medium heat. Stir in xylitol, milks, celtic sea salt, and xanthan gum.

2. Cook, stirring constantly. Bring to a boil and boil for 2 minutes.

3. Remove from heat and stir in the almond butter, vanilla extract and almond extract.

4. Pour into a mixing bowl. Add powdered xylitol and stevia to taste - a little at a time until just a bit too sweet (the sweetness dulls when freezing). Mix until creamy and smooth.

5. Pour into a greased 8x8 baking pan. Chill until firm (in the fridge or freezer).

6. Store in the fridge.

*For Stage 2:

• be cautious with butter for the first two weeks.

**you can replace this with an allowed nut butter of choice; but be aware it may change the flavor.

CHOCOLATE COMA FUDGE

"When my husband bit into these, his eyes got wide. 'These are a perfect 10!'" ~ Paula

Allowed on:

Stage 2 - *notes below   Stage 3

Ingredients

- 1 c. cocoa butter
- 1 1/2 sticks butter
- 1 c. raw cacao powder
- ¾ c. xylitol granules
- a few pinches of salt
- 1 ½ tsp. vanilla
- stevia to taste

Directions

1. In a medium saucepan heat cocoa butter and butter until melted. Add cacao powder, xylitol, and salt. Simmer and stir until xylitol is dissolved.

2. Remove from heat and add vanilla. Add stevia to taste - a little at a time.

3. Pour into an 8x8 greased with coconut oil or butter. Refrigerate 1-2 hours or until set. Cut into small squares as these are very rich.

4. Keep stored in refrigerator.

*For Stage 2:

• avoid cocoa butter and cacao powder for the first two weeks.

• be cautious with butter for the first two weeks.

"BEST THING EVER" ALMOND BUTTER BUCKEYES

"My friend Annemarie sent me a text while placing her Azure Standard order and mentioned she was getting almond butter. She said, 'I never gave a rip about almond butter until I tried your buckeyes!' According to her they are, 'the best thing ever!'" ~ Sarah

Allowed on:

> Stage 2 - *notes below   Stage 3

Ingredients

(makes 20 pieces)

center:

- 1/2 c. butter, softened
- 3/4 c. raw almond butter**
- 1 tsp. vanilla extract
- pinch of celtic sea salt
- 1/2 c. xylitol granules
- 1/2 tsp. cinnamon, optional

chocolate coating:

- 1/2 c. coconut oil
- 1/4 c. raw cacao powder
- pinch of celtic sea salt
- stevia to taste

optional chocolate coating:

- Homemade Chocolate Chips/Chunks, still warm and melted

Directions

1. In a medium mixing bowl, combine xylitol/cinnamon with butter, almond butter, vanilla extract, and salt and mix on medium speed until well incorporated.

2. Use a small scoop, or form balls in your hand, and place on a parchment lined baking sheet. Freeze for about 20 minutes.

3. In the meantime, put coconut oil in a small pan and melt. Add the rest of the ingredients (add stevia a little at a time) and stir well. Let cool. Remove baking sheet from freezer and dip the centers in the coating. Put back in freezer for about 5 minutes.

4. Repeat 2 more times to make a nice coating. Store in freezer.

*For Stage 2:

• avoid cocoa butter and cacao powder for the first two weeks.

• be cautious with butter for the first two weeks.

**you can replace this with an allowed nut butter of choice; but be aware it may change the flavor.

WHATEVER YOUR FANCY TRUFFLES

Allowed on:

Stage 2 - *notes below   Stage 3

Ingredients

- 1 - 15 oz can of black beans, drained and rinsed
- 3 Tbs. coconut oil, soft but not melted
- 1 tsp. vanilla extract
- ¼ c. raw cacao powder
- 2 pinches of celtic sea salt
- stevia to taste

optional:

- peppermint, orange, lemon, etc. extract to taste
- raw cacao powder, for rolling the truffles in
- finely chopped nuts, for rolling the truffles in

Directions

1. Put all ingredients, including optional extract, into a blender or food processor and blend well (until there are no chunks of bean). Remember to add stevia a little at a time until just a bit too sweet (the sweetness dulls when frozen).

2. Take a small amount of dough into your hands and roll into balls. If desired, roll in raw cacao powder or nuts.

3. Put onto a small baking dish or tray and freeze for approximately 30 minutes to firm up.

4. You can store in the freezer or fridge. If you store in the freezer, remove for a bit before serving.

*For Stage 2:

- avoid cacao powder for the first two weeks.

SEA SALT CHOCOLATE ALMOND CLUSTERS

"Oh, my taste buds....YUM! I'm sitting here nibbling on it while I write this. The addition of the course sea salt? Awesome! I love the salty taste combined with the dark chocolate and the crunch of the almonds. I think the salt cut through the bitterness of the cocoa and I used coconut flavored coconut oil and that added flavor was awesome. I love this recipe!" ~ Tracy

Allowed on:

Stage 2 - *notes below   Stage 3

Ingredients

- 1 c. coconut oil
- 1/2 c. raw cacao powder
- 1/4 tsp. fine celtic sea salt
- 1/2 tsp. vanilla extract
- stevia to taste
- raw almonds
- coarse celtic sea salt

Directions

1. Place 5 almonds in each cup of a mini muffin pan.

2. In a small saucepan, melt coconut oil. Stir in raw cacao powder, fine celtic sea salt, and vanilla extract. Add stevia to taste - a little at a time until just a bit too sweet (the sweetness dulls when freezing).

3. Pour chocolate mixture over almonds, dividing it evenly between each muffin hole.

4. Freeze for a couple of minutes until just a little solid and then sprinkle each cup with a small amount of coarse celtic sea salt.

5. Store in the freezer.

*For Stage 2:

• avoid cacao powder for the first two weeks.

FREEZER FRIEND MELT-IN-YOUR-MOUTH MINTS

"I wish these were vegetables, then you would feed them to us all the time." ~ Luke, 5 yrs. old

Allowed on:

> Stage 1   Stage 2 - *notes below   Stage 3

Ingredients

- 4 Tbs. (2 ozs.) cream cheese
- 1/4 c. powdered xylitol
- 1/4 tsp. peppermint extract
- stevia to taste
- 2-3 drops of food coloring (optional)

Directions

1. Beat all of the above ingredients in a small mixing bowl. Add stevia to taste - a little at a time.

2. Scoop mixture into a decorating bag and pipe tiny mints onto a baking sheet lined with parchment paper.

3. Put mints into freezer right away and only remove when you're ready to eat them.

Sarah's note:

These mints need to live in your freezer. They will start to melt within minutes of being out of the freezer.

*For Stage 2:

• cream cheese is not allowed for the first two weeks.

SHORTBREAD CARAMEL SQUARES/CANDY BARS

"When you gotta have a Twix. . ." ~ Paula

Allowed on:

Stage 2 - *notes below   Stage 3

Ingredients

shortbread cookie crust:

- 2 c. almond flour, packed
- 1 tsp. baking soda
- 1/2 tsp. celtic sea salt
- 5 Tbs. butter, softened
- 1 T. vanilla extract
- 1/2 tsp. almond extract
- stevia to taste

caramel:

- 1/2 of a All of Your Caramel Dreams Come True recipe brought to hard ball stage.

topping:

- one Homemade Chocolate Chips/Chunks recipe, still warm and melted

Directions

1. Preheat oven to 350 degrees. Line a 9x9 pan with parchment paper, leaving about 2" up the sides. Lightly grease with butter or coconut oil.

2. Combine almond flour, baking soda, and celtic sea salt. Cut butter into flour with pastry cutter.

3. Add vanilla and almond extracts and stir until well combined. The consistency should be crumbly, but hold together if you form it into a ball. Add stevia to taste - a little at a time until just a bit too sweet (the sweetness dulls when baking).

4. Press crust into pan. Bake for 15 minutes until lightly browned. Cool completely.

5. For the caramel, make half the recipe as directed, bringing it to the hardball stage. Pour over cooled shortbread cookie crust and refrigerate until hardened.

6. For the coating, make a full recipe of Homemade Chocolate Chips/Chunks - but do not refrigerate, keep them melted.

7. To make into squares, pour the chocolate chips overtop the hardened caramel and place pan in refrigerator to harden. Before cutting into squares, let soften just a little so the chocolate coating doesn't crack.

8. To make into candy bars, pull the cookie/caramel crust out of the pan with the edges of the parchment paper. Gently flip over on a baking sheet so the caramel layer is on the bottom. With a sharp knife, carefully cut into rectangular bars. Dip each bar into the melted chocolate chips and set back onto the parchment paper. Refrigerate to harden.

9. Keep refrigerated.

Paula's note:

These are super rich and sweet. Eat accordingly. :)

*For Stage 2:

• avoid cacao powder and cocoa butter (in Homemade Chocolate Chips/Chunks) for the first two weeks.

• use butter with caution for the first two weeks.

ALL OF YOUR CARAMEL DREAMS COME TRUE

Allowed on:

Stage 1   Stage 2 - *notes below   Stage 3

Ingredients

- 1 c. butter
- 2 c. xylitol granules
- 1/2 tsp. celtic sea salt
- 1/2 tsp. xanthan gum
- 1 tsp. vanilla extract
- 1/2 tsp. baking soda

Directions

1. Melt butter in a medium pot. Stir in xylitol, salt, xanthan gum, and vanilla extract.

2. Cook - stirring constantly until hard ball stage on a candy thermometer (or when you drip some of the caramel in cold water it quickly becomes a ball). Remove from heat and stir in baking soda.

3. Then get creative! Drizzle it over popcorn and bake at low temperature for about 30 minutes for caramel corn. Pour into a small pan, chill, and cut into rectangles or squares for cute caramels. Let chill and then wrap it around apples for caramel apples. Use it in all sorts of treats!

4. Be sure to keep anything made with this caramel (except the popcorn) stored in the freezer so that it will stay firm. It should be eaten within a few days.

*For Stage 2:

• use butter with caution for the first two weeks.

PERFECTLY PLAYFUL MARZIPAN

Allowed on:

Stage 1   Stage 2 - *notes below   Stage 3

Ingredients

- 1 1/2 c. fine almond flour
- 1/2 c. powdered xylitol
- a good splash of almond extract
- 1 egg white
- stevia to taste
- food coloring (optional)

Directions

1. Put all the ingredients in the blender or food processor and pulse until well combined.

2. Pour the mix on an almond floured board and knead. It will be sticky, so add more almond flour until it's nice and pliable (and easy to mold).

3. If you'd like different colors, divide into bowls and add drops of food coloring and knead with your hands until desired color is reached. Shape into desired shapes.

4. Store in the fridge.

Sarah's note:

If you don't have fine almond flour, put it in a blender or food processor and pulse until nice and fine. Do not over grind because you'll end up with almond butter instead.

*For Stage 2:

• avoid egg whites for the first two weeks.

SWEET & SPEEDY SNACKS

CINNAMON & SUGAR NUTS

Allowed on:

Stage 1   Stage 2 - *notes below   Stage 3

Ingredients

- 1 tsp. melted butter or coconut oil
- 1 tsp. cinnamon
- 1/4 tsp. celtic sea salt
- stevia to taste
- 1 c. nuts of choice (fresh or presoaked and dehydrated)

Directions

1. In a small saucepan, melt butter or coconut oil and stir in spices.

2. Add stevia to taste - a little at a time until just a bit too sweet (the sweetness dulls when baking).

3. Stir in nuts until well coated.

4. Dehydrate at 150 degrees or bake in oven at 350 until dried and crunchy.

*For Stage 2:

- use butter with caution for the first two weeks (or substitute with coconut oil).

HOLIDAY SPICED NUTS

Allowed on:

Stage 1   Stage 2 - *notes below   Stage 3

Ingredients

- 1 tsp. melted butter or coconut oil
- 1 Tbs. xylitol granules
- 1/4 tsp. vanilla extract
- 1/2 tsp. cinnamon
- 1/4 tsp. allspice
- 1/8 tsp. cloves
- 1/8 tsp. nutmeg
- 1/2 tsp. celtic sea salt
- stevia to taste
- 1 c. nuts of choice (fresh or presoaked and dehydrated)

Directions

1. In a small saucepan, melt butter or coconut oil and stir in spices.

2. Add stevia to taste - a little at a time until just a bit too sweet (the sweetness dulls when baking).

3. Stir in nuts until well coated.

4. Dehydrate at 150 degrees or bake in oven at 350 until dried and crunchy.

*For Stage 2:

• use butter with caution for the first two weeks (or substitute with coconut oil).

SWEET & SPICY NUTS

Allowed on:

Stage 1   Stage 2 - *notes below   Stage 3

Ingredients

- 1 tsp. melted butter or coconut oil
- 1/4 tsp. celtic sea salt
- 1/8 tsp. pepper
- 1/4 tsp. cinnamon
- 1/4 tsp. allspice
- 1/4 tsp. cumin
- 1/8 tsp. cayenne pepper
- 1/2 tsp. rosemary
- stevia to taste
- 1 c. nuts of choice (fresh or presoaked and dehydrated)

Directions

1. In a small saucepan, melt butter or coconut oil and stir in spices.
2. Add stevia to taste - a little at a time until just a bit too sweet (the sweetness dulls when baking).
3. Stir in nuts until well coated.
4. Dehydrate at 150 degrees or bake in oven at 350 until dried and crunchy.

*For Stage 2:

• use butter with caution for the first two weeks (or substitute with coconut oil).

WHATEVER YOU'RE CRAVING KETTLE CORN

"One of our mainstay family night treats that satisfies the craving for a sweet and salty snack." ~ Paula

Allowed on:

> Stage 2 - *notes below   Stage 3

Ingredients

- 8 c. air-popped popcorn
- 1 Tbs. butter, melted
- 1/4 tsp. celtic sea salt
- stevia to taste

Directions

1. Drizzle popcorn with butter. Shake on celtic sea salt and stir. Lightly sprinkle stevia to taste.

*For Stage 2:

- avoid corn for the first two weeks.
- use butter with caution for the first two weeks (or substitute with coconut oil).

PERSONAL SIZE LEMON MACADAMIA YOGURT DELICHT

Allowed on:

Stage 1   Stage 2 - *notes below   Stage 3

Ingredients

- 1 1/2 c. of plain greek yogurt
- 2 Tbs. of lemon juice (or to taste - 2 Tbs. will make it really tart)
- a small pinch of celtic sea salt
- 1 1/4 tsp. vanilla extract
- stevia to taste
- a small handful of macadamia nuts, roughly chopped

Directions

1. Stir all ingredients together in a bowl and serve.

2. Remember to add stevia a little at a time.

*For Stage 2:

• greek yogurt is not allowed for the first two weeks.

PHONY BLUEBERRY PIE

Allowed on:

Stage 2   Stage 3

Ingredients

- 1 c. of blueberries
- dash of vanilla extract
- pinch of celtic sea salt
- 1/4 c. of vanilla almond milk (adjust to your preference)
- stevia to taste

Directions

1. *Speedy Version:* Put all ingredients in a bowl and microwave for about a minute.
2. *Purist Version:* Put all ingredients in a pot on the stove and cook until the berries are heated through.

APPLE CINNAMON OATMEAL DESSERT

"The oatmeal turned out great. Just the right texture of oatmeal and apple with the perfect amount of sweetness." Jennifer, Owen Family Six

Allowed on:

Stage 2 - *notes below   Stage 3

Ingredients

- 2 c. cooked oatmeal
- 1 chopped green apple
- cinnamon to taste
- stevia to taste
- tad bit of butter

Directions

1. Cook oatmeal on the stovetop according to directions.
2. Add apple, cinnamon, stevia, and butter and stir until the apples are tender. Remember to add stevia just a little at a time.

*For Stage 2:

• be cautious with oats and butter (or try substituting with coconut oil) for the first two weeks.

QUENCH YOUR CRAVINGS: DESSERTS YOU CAN DRINK

///

CANDIDA KILLER TEA

///

Allowed on:

| Stage 1 | Stage 2 | Stage 3 |

Ingredients

- 4 Tbs. Pau D'Arco bark
- 2 Tbs. alfalfa leaves (optional)
- 4 c. water
- 1/2 c. almond milk
- 2 pinches celtic sea salt
- 2 tsp. vanilla extract
- stevia
- dash of cayenne

Directions

1. Put the Pau D'Arco bark, alfalfa, and water in a pot and boil for 20 minutes. (You can also put the leaves in your glass coffee pot and let the 4 cups of water run through the empty coffee maker.) Let it cool and then strain.

2. Take 2 cups of the finished tea and add 1/2 c. almond milk, 2 pinches of celtic sea salt, 2 tsp. vanilla extract, stevia to taste, and a tiny dash of cayenne.

3. Fill a quart jar or large glass with ice to the top. Pour the tea mix over the ice. The ice will melt a little - fill the jar the rest of the way to the top with water.

4. Refrigerate the other 2 cups of unused tea for another glass later.

Sarah's Busy Morning Version

1. Pour 2 c. brewed Pau D'Arco tea into a 1/2 gallon mason jar filled with ice.

2. Fill almost to the top with almond milk, 2 pinches of celtic sea salt, stevia to

taste, and 2 tsp. of vanilla extract.

Paula's Mega Version *(for a 1 gallon jar)*

- 1 c. Pau D' Arco bark
- 1/2 c. alfalfa leaves
- 4 c. water
- 8 pinches celtic sea salt
- 1 Tbs. vanilla extract
- stevia to taste
- 8 dashes cayenne
- almond milk as needed

1. Put the Pau D'Arco bark and alfalfa an empty glass coffee pot and run the 4 cups of water through the coffee maker. Let it cool and then strain the bark and leaves out.

2. Pour all of the tea into a glass gallon jar, add the salt, vanilla, stevia, and cayenne. Fill the jar to the top with water.

3. To drink, fill a quart jar or large glass with ice. Fill about ¾ full with the tea mix and then top it off with almond milk. Add stevia to taste.

ALMOND & VANILLA SWIRL FRAPPUCCINO

"I can't tell you how much the swirl makes me smile.
I LOVE this drink!" ~ Paula

Allowed on:

Stage **1**   Stage **2**   Stage **3**

Ingredients

- 2 c. fresh brewed decaffeinated coffee
- ice
- almond milk
- 1 tsp. vanilla extract
- 2 pinches celtic sea salt
- stevia to taste

Directions

1. Fill 1/2 gallon jar with ice. Pour in 2 c. fresh brewed decaf coffee. Add more ice to bring back to top.
2. Fill almost to rim with almond milk. Add vanilla extract, celtic sea salt, and stevia.

CHOCOLATE–COVERED MINT COFFEE

Allowed on:

Stage 2 - *notes below   Stage 3

Ingredients

- 2 c. decaffeinated coffee
- 1 T. raw cocoa powder
- 2 c. almond milk
- ice
- a few drops peppermint extract
- 1/2 tsp. vanilla extract
- 1/4-½ tsp. chocolate extract
- pinch of celtic sea salt
- stevia to taste

Directions

1. Pour two cups of hot coffee into a 1/2 gallon jar. Add raw cocoa powder, extracts and sea salt and stir until the cocoa powder is dissolved.
2. Add to ice to the top of the jar. Add almond milk and stevia to taste. Stir well and enjoy!

Sarah's note:

Start with just a drop of peppermint extract and add drops to desired flavor.

*For Stage 2:

• avoid cacao powder for the first two weeks.

WANNABE COCONUT FRAPPUCCINO

"WARNING: May cause brain freeze. Use straw!" ~ Sarah

Allowed on:

Stage 2 - *notes below   Stage 3

Ingredients

- 1 c. almond milk
- 1/4 c. decaffeinated coffee
- 2 c. ice
- 1/3 c. Homemade Chocolate Chips/Chunks
- 1/2 c. shredded coconut
- 1 tsp. vanilla extract
- 1/4 tsp. almond extract
- pinch of celtic sea salt
- stevia to taste

Directions:

1. Put all ingredients in a blender and blend well.
2. Add more stevia, ice or almond milk to desired sweetness and thickness.

*For Stage 2:

• avoid cacao powder and cocoa butter (in Homemade Chocolate Chips/Chunks) for the first two weeks.

BLUEBERRY ALMOND CHIA SMOOTHIE

Allowed on:

Stage 2 - *notes below   Stage 3

Ingredients

- 1/2 c. almond milk
- 1 c. blueberries
- a handful of spinach
- 1 tsp. chia seeds
- 1/2 ripe avocado
- stevia to taste
- 1/2-1 tsp. raw apple cider vinegar
- a good sprinkle of cinnamon
- 1 - 1 1/2 c. ice

Directions

1. Throw everything except the ice into a high-powered blender. Start low and go high.
2. Once it's well blended, add ice and blend again to desired consistency.

PERFECTLY PUMPKIN PIE SMOOTHIE

Allowed on:

Stage 2 - *notes below   Stage 3

Ingredients

- 1 1/2 c. almond milk
- 3/4 c. pumpkin puree
- 1/2 tsp. vanilla
- 1/2 tsp. cinnamon
- 1/8 tsp. ginger
- dash of allspice
- 1/4 tsp. nutmeg
- dash of cardamom
- dash of cloves
- 2 Tbs. flax meal
- 1 tsp. chia seeds
- 2 Tbs. raw almond butter**
- 1/4 tsp. celtic sea salt
- 1 tsp. blackstrap molasses
- approximately 2 cups of ice
- stevia to taste

Directions

1. Combine all ingredients except ice into a blender and blend until well incorporated.
2. Add ice to desired thickness and stevia to desired sweetness.

*For Stage 2:

• avoid molasses for the first two weeks.

**you can replace this with an allowed nut butter of choice; but be aware it may change the flavor

WARM AND COZY TURMERIC MILK

"This drink is surprisingly tasty and REALLY good for pain and your metabolism. This works better for me than Ibuprofen!" ~ Sarah

Allowed on:

Stage 1   Stage 2   Stage 3

Ingredients

- 1 c. almond milk
- 1 c. water
- 1-2 inches of fresh turmeric, cut into little slices
- 3 peppercorns
- 1 t. of cardamon powder (I tried the pods and really prefer the flavor of the ground cardamon, but you can use 3 pods instead)
- ½-1 inch of fresh ginger, cut into slices
- 1 Tbs. coconut oil
- a tiny shake of cayenne
- a good shake of cinnamon
- stevia to taste

Directions

1. Put all ingredients into a pot and let simmer for a few minutes (the milk should turn slightly orange). Once hot, strain and drink.

MISCELLANEOUS MORSELS

HOMEMADE CHOCOLATE CHIPS/CHUNKS

Allowed on:

Stage 2 - *notes below   Stage 3

Ingredients

- 1 c. cocoa butter
- 1 c. raw cacao powder
- 1 tsp. vanilla extract
- 1/8 tsp. almond extract
- 1 T. butter, optional if casein-free
- 1 Tbs. xylitol granules
- pinch of celtic sea salt
- stevia to taste

Directions

1. Melt the cocoa butter over low heat in a small saucepan.
2. Add the cacao powder, vanilla extract, almond extract, butter, and xylitol.
3. Add stevia to taste - just a little at a time.
4. Bring to a light, simmering boil and then remove from heat. Let it cool a bit.

5. You can use this as a dip or to pour over chocolate-covered candies.

6. To make chocolate chips, let cool until it seems like it would start to keep form. Scoop into a decorating bag and pipe small chips onto a parchment lined baking sheet. Refrigerate or freeze until hardened.

7. If you want a quicker version (chocolate chunks), pour the melted mixture into a 9x9 glass pan and refrigerate until hardened. Break apart into small chunks with a knife and store in the fridge or freezer.

8. These will hold up to baking if you add them to cookies, bars, etc.

*For Stage 2:

• avoid cacao powder and cocoa butter for the first two weeks.

• use butter with caution for the first two weeks.

CHIA EGGS

(replaces 1 egg)

Allowed on:

Stage 1   Stage 2   Stage 3

Ingredients

- 1 Tbs. ground chia seeds
- 3 Tbs. warm water

Directions:

1. In a coffee grinder or high-powered blender, grind the chia seeds to a fine powder.
2. Pour the seed powder into a small bowl and let it sit about five minutes until it gets like egg white consistency.
3. Use in place of eggs in any baked goods.

PART THREE:

Truly, truly, I say to you, whoever believes has eternal life. I am the bread of life. Your fathers ate the manna in the wilderness, and they died. This is the bread that comes down from heaven, so that one may eat of it and not die.

John 6: 47-50

EXCERPTS FROM HEALING CANDIDA WITH FOOD

(available in PDF form)

CANDIDA

Have you ever gone to the doctor for a specific issue (or multiple issues) and been told it's all in your head? **Or, have they listened to your concerns only to hand you a prescription for creams, drugs, steroids, and other quick fixes?** Perhaps those treatments relieved your discomfort for a while - but has it come back? Have you suddenly realized that several years have gone by and you're not any better?

Have you ever been on antibiotics? Have you taken the Pill? Do you have recurring vaginal yeast infections? Does your baby have a diaper rash that never goes away? Do you have psoriasis? Does your back, chest, or abdomen get dry red or white patches? Do you have a nail fungus? Do you struggle with jock itch? Does your little one have cradle cap or thrush? Are you moody and irritable? Do you have recurring diarrhea or constipation? Have you been diagnosed with IBS? Do you have a child considered autistic or labelled as ADHD or ADD?

Why all the questions? Because believe it or not, **they all have something in common.**

Candida.

WHAT IS CANDIDA?

I'm assuming that since you're reading this, you probably already have a basic idea of what candida is. If not, let me lay it out for you in my favorite terms: layman's terms.

Candida albicans is a toxic, yeast-like organism that everyone has in their digestive system. If it's kept in balance by good bacteria, it's generally harmless. However, when your immune system becomes weakened, candida mutates, takes over your body, and becomes a serious condition called systematic candidiasis or more commonly, candida. **Sounds like a bad sci-fi movie, doesn't it.**

When candida starts to spread out of control, it begins to appear in different ways. Some are not visible: irritation, moodiness, ADHD, stomach and digestive issues, while others are seen quite obviously as skin rashes, thrush, yeast infections (in both men and women), diaper rash, cradle cap, athlete's foot, jock itch, etc.

Candida is underrated. Like. . .a lot underrated. Not only does it cause an alarming number of symptoms, it's also a pre-cursor to auto-immune diseases and some would go so far as to say cancer.

SYMPTOMS OF CANDIDA

Symptoms, then are in reality nothing butthe cry from suffering organs.

~ Jean Martin Charcot, translated from French

(this is not an exhaustive list - trust me, there's more)

• acne	• heart burn
• anxiety	• heart palpitations
• arthritis	• hypoglycemia (low blood sugar)
• asthma	• hypothyroidism
• athletes' foot	• insomnia
• brain fog	• irritability
• cold hands or feet	• joint pain
• colds	• lack of appetite
• colic	• migraines
• constipation	• mood swings
• cradle cap	• muscle aches and pain
• cravings for sweets	• panic attacks
• cysts	• poor memory and concentration
• diabetes	• pre-menstrual syndrome (PMS)
• diaper rash	• psoriasis
• diarrhea	• rashes and dry red or white patches
• dizziness	• respiratory problems
• eczema	• sinus congestion
• fatigue	• thrush (white coating in mouth or vagina)
• food sensitivities or reactions	
• hay fever	
• headaches	

Most conventional doctors don't know a lot about candida and often misdiagnose it or wave it aside as a fad. But there are other doctors, naturopaths, and herbalists who believe it is the root of many hard-to-diagnose chronic illnesses. **These are the doctors I encourage you to see - those that get to the root of the problem instead of shoveling dirt on top of it.**

WHAT CONTRIBUTES TO CANDIDA?

Sugar is a type of bodily fuel, yes,

but your body runs about as well on it as a car would.

~ V.L. Allineare

- antacids
- antibiotics
- anti-inflammatory drugs
- anti-ulcer medications
- carbohydrates
- environmental toxins
- foods with starch
- foods with yeast
- hormone replacement therapy
- oral contraceptives
- over-the-counter medicines
- prescription drugs
- radiation
- smoking
- steroids
- sugar in all forms

To find out if you have candida, take a simple blood test you can do in the comfort of your home, or try the Yeast Infection Evaluation Test - an online quiz created by Dr. Eric Bakker, ND, a naturopathic doctor who treats candida patients. You can specify the test for men, women, or children.

WHAT STEPS SHOULD I TAKE?

In order to change we must be sick and tired of being sick and tired.

~Author Unknown

You've already taken the first step. If you're reading this it's because you're ready to become proactive in your battle with candida. **Changing your diet is one of THE most important steps you can take.**

The other step, and just as important, is to start treating your candida with natural remedies and specific anti-candida supplements rather than creams, drugs, and prescriptions. In fact, those only encourage candida to grow.

A good healing protocol will be 80% diet and 20% supplements.

The ebook, Candida Crusher, written by naturopath Dr. Eric Bakker, who's been treating candida for over 20 years, is the most comprehensive, yet easy to understand book I've read on candida. It's filled with case studies, step-by-step instructions on herbal remedies and supplements, and an overall health guide that will tell you how to crush candida once and for all. I highly recommend it.

Disclaimer: Candida Crusher is a medical volume and contains anatomical photos that some readers may find objectionable.

HOW LONG TO HEAL?

This is a common question and it varies greatly from one source to another and from one person to another. Most often it depends on how long you've had candida and its severity. Some sources will say a minimum of four weeks while others say a month for every year you've been sick. **They all agree however, that if you leave it unchecked, it will only get worse.**

I've found Dr. Bakker's estimation to be most accurate. He has seen literally thousands of patients heal from candida and estimates that it can take a few months to a year or more. In my own personal experience it took Travis and I between 9-12 months. **Again, it depends on the severity of your candida and how closely you follow a healing protocol.**

THE THREE-STAGE DIET

If you've been on a very poor diet, I recommend first doing the 7-day Big Clean-Up plan. It will help your transition to Stage One by decreasing your physical and mental discomfort. You can find the details to the Big Clean-Up in Candida Crusher.

During all three stages I encourage you to purchase organic and/or non-GMO foods if at all possible. Look for meat that doesn't have antibiotics. Some will specify no added antibiotics or growth hormones, but that just means they didn't **add** any. If the animal's feed had it in there, then they have it in their meat and body fat. **Antibiotics in any form are one of the biggest contributors to candida.**

STAGE 1: M.E.V.Y.

(approx. 2-3 weeks)
This stage is the 'induction' stage. The acronym stands for

Meat

Eggs

Vegetables

Yogurt

It's critical that you stick to this stage like the superglue you used to stick your fingers together when you were a kid. (C'mon - we all did that!)

In this stage you're allowed to eat all meats and seafood, eggs, most all vegetables (except the ones high in starches like potatoes, sweet potato, carrots, pumpkin, peas, corn, and beets) and plain, natural unsweetened acidophilus yogurt. No other dairy is allowed unless it's sour cream or cream cheese made from the yogurt. No fruits. Stevia and xylitol are the only allowed sweeteners.

You can have naturally fermented foods like kim-chi, sauerkraut, kefir, whey, and Bragg's apple cider vinegar.

You will need to avoid all store-bought breads (they contain yeasts and sugars), but pure sourdough bread (no commercial yeast added) is okay. If you want to be a little stricter and really kick it into gear, I'd avoid even sourdough breads during these few weeks.

So how do you know if you should follow this stage for two or three weeks? Dr.

Bakker says a bare minimum of two weeks, but preferably three. He suggests that **when you don't seem to be improving anymore**, that's when to move to Stage Two. I know, that doesn't really make sense, but trust me, when you read Stage Two you'll understand.

STAGE 1 ALLOWED FOODS:

Fats	Animal Fats	Protein
• almond oil • coconut oil • macadamia oil • olive oil • palm oil/shortening • peanut oil • sesame oil • sunflower oil • walnut oil	• butter or ghee • fat from meat and fish • lard • bacon fat (from bacon with no added sugar or nitrates) • cod liver oil	• eggs • all red meat • all poultry • all fish • all shellfish

Vegetables		
• asparagus • artichoke • beans (green and wax) • bok choy • bamboo shoots • broccoli • brussels sprouts • cabbage • cauliflower • celery • celery root (celeriac) • cucumbers • eggplant	• fennel • garlic • ginger • horseradish • jicama • kohlrabi • leeks • okra • onions • greens (green leaf lettuce; head lettuce has no nutritional value, spinach, chard, collards, mustard greens, kale, radicchio, endive, etc.)	• peppers (all bell peppers) • radishes • rutabagas • scallions and green onions • sea vegetables (nori, kombu, wakame, etc.) • snow peas, snap peas, pea pods • spaghetti squash • sprouts (bean, alfalfa, etc) • summer squash • tomatoes • tomatillos • turnips • watercress • zucchini (courgette)

Nuts & Seeds	Fruit	Herbs & Misc.
• almonds • Brazil nuts • cashews (susceptible to mold) • hazelnuts • macadamia nuts • walnuts • flax seed (flax meal) • sunflower seeds • pumpkin seeds • sesame seeds • coconut flour • almond flour Make sure your nuts are properly soaked and dried for easier digestion.	• lemons • limes	• all dried and fresh herbs • nutritional yeast • mushrooms - ONLY if soaked overnight in extra virgin olive oil and fresh garlic.

Dairy	Beverages	Fermented	Sweeteners
• butter • buttermilk • hard cheeses like cheddar, colby, Parmesan, Swiss MAY be okay, but if in doubt don't eat them for this stage • sour cream (with live cultures*) or replace with greek yogurt with live cultures* • cream cheese with live cultures* • yogurt (make your own or look for unpasteurized, unsweetened yogurt that features 'live active cultures*' or 'living cultures*') *if you can't find a product with 'live cultures' the next best option would be to add a probiotic capsule to it.	• almond milk • coconut milk • decaf coffee • non-caffeinated herbal teas (especially Pau d' arco) • water	• apple cider vinegar • kefir • kim-chi • sauerkraut • whey	• stevia • xylitol

STAGE 2: LOW-ALLERGY FOODS

(approx. 2-6 weeks)

Have you been told you're allergic or intolerant to certain foods? Stage Two cleans up your diet by eliminating the foods you know or suspect you have troubles with.

In this stage you're going to want to steer clear of any foods that have high allergenic potential. Foods high on the allergy list like milk products, gluten, peanuts, etc. damage your immune system and give candida the upper hand.

Avoid these foods - and don't introduce them back in too soon in Stage Three or you'll just add fuel to candida's fire. In other words, candida will really, really like you - but not in a good way.

You will continue to eat most of the foods allowed on the MEVY diet, with just a little more wiggle room in some areas and a little less in others. Please don't trick yourself into thinking you can skip this stage, your recovery will suffer for it.

So why remove these foods in Stage Two instead of Stage One? Short answer: eliminating sugar, yeast, carbs, and starting a new diet is stress enough on a person - sometimes taking away foods you're sensitive to can cause discomfort as well. A careful approach is much better for you and the loved ones who have to live with you. ;)

Make sure you're drinking water with fresh lemon juice to help with detoxing.

STAGE 2 ALLOWED/NOT ALLOWED FOODS:

Stage 2 KEY for the not allowed/avoid list in the right column:

bold foods = these food are not allowed for at least 2 weeks. If you're severely affected with candida, have known food allergies, or strongly react to foods in your diet, then Dr. Bakker suggests that you also **avoid the *italics and underlined foods* for the first two weeks as well. It doesn't mean you can't have them at all, just avoid having them too much.**

plain font foods = these foods are listed because they have a tendency to create reactions. However, you should not have to avoid them altogether. If you don't have reactions to them or had a low candida test score, you can certainly eat them. We do suggest that you **use caution and avoid them if you had a** high testing score **and/or have a severe case of candida.**

We refer to the first two weeks of Stage 2 as 2a because you'll need to show extra caution and closely follow the not allowed/avoid list very carefully.

After that initial 2 weeks you move to the second half of Stage 2 - what we like to call 2b. In 2b you slowly start allowing the underlined foods a little more, while avoiding the bold foods. It's kind of like the bold foods move to underlined foods, the underlined foods graduate to plain font . . . the idea is to be very careful and only add foods gradually. If you seem to have a reaction, then back off for awhile.

Food Groups	Allowed	Not Allowed/Avoid
Proteins	• chicken • fish (unless you know you have an allergy) • turkey • venison • all dried beans • dried peas • lentils	• _eggs (white & yolk)_ • _fish and shellfish_ • _lamb_ • _red meats_ • _soy products_ • canned meats • cold cuts • corned beef • egg substitutes • pork • processed meats in general • sausage
Dairy	• almond milk • coconut milk • oat milk • rice milk	• **cheese** • **cottage cheese** • **cream** • **ice cream** • **milk** • **non-dairy creamer** • **yogurt**
Starches	• amaranth • arrowroot • buckwheat • millet • rice • tapioca • sweet potato • quinoa	• _all gluten-containing products (including pasta)_ • _corn_ • corn containing products

Breads & Cereals	• any flat bread made from 100% certified gluten-free: • almond flour • amaranth • arrowroot • buckwheat • coconut flour • millet • potato flour • rice • tapioca • sweet potato • quinoa	• Any bread (containing sugars and yeast) made from: • _barley_ • _rye_ • _spelt_ • _wheat_ • '_Gluten-Free_' containing breads • _sourdough bread_ - still exercise extreme caution if you have chronic yeast issues • kamut • oats
Vegetables	• all vegetables	• creamed vegetables or those made with prohibited ingredients.
Fruits	• avocado • blueberries • coconut • green apples (generally OK)	• **banana** • **oranges** • _pineapple_ • cocktails • fruit drinks • all dried fruits • dried fruit preservatives with sulphites
Soups	• clear, vegetable based broth from scratch	• **canned or creamed soups** • soups with glutinous flours & grains

Beverages	• herbal teas (unsweetened) • Pau d'arco tea • water with lemon juice • water with 5 drops grapefruit seed extract per 250 mls of water	**• milk or milk-based drinks** **• orange juice** • _kombucha_ (this might be a bit risky unless your candida is quite minor. If the kombucha ferment has not properly "set", you could be consuming too much sugar and could potentially have a huge setback.) • alcoholic drinks • most citrus drinks • dairy based drinks • diet drinks • energy drinks
Oils & Fats	• cold pressed oils, preferably in dark amber bottles: • coconut oil • grape seed oil • linseed oil • olive oil • oregano oil • palm oil/shortening • pumpkin oil • sesame oil • sunflower oil • walnut oil	• butter • deep-fried foods • margarines • salad dressings • shortening/lard • spreads (sugars) • vegetable oil blends
Nuts & Seeds	• almonds • brazil nuts • hazelnuts • walnuts • pecans • flax seed (flax meal) • pumpkin seeds • sesame seeds • sunflower • squash seeds • nut/seed butter made with allowed ingredients - watch those sugars.	**• peanuts** **• peanut butter** • _cacao powder_ • cashew nuts • pistachios • hazelnut spread (sugar)

Sweeteners & Treats	• stevia • xylitol • in small amounts: • brown rice syrup • fruit sweeteners	• **chocolate** • _raw cacao powder_ • _all types of sugar:_ • _brown sugar_ • _cane sugar_ • _caster_ • _corn syrup_ • _Demerara_ • _dextrose_ • _fructose_ • _glucose_ • _honey_ • _icing_ • _malt_ • _maple syrup_ • _molasses_ • _white sugar_
Herbs & Misc	• all dried and fresh herbs • nutritional yeast • mushrooms - ONLY if soaked overnight in extra virgin olive oil and fresh garlic.	

STAGE 3: RE-INTRODUCTION

Once you start to feel really (and I mean really) good, you can start Stage Three. In this reintroduction stage you can eat foods from both Stage One and Two while _slowly_ reintroducing the foods from the 'not allowed/avoid' list on Stage Two.

Start by reintroducing foods with the least amount of sugar or starch. Add back one food at a time and each food over a three-day period. For instance, if you want to add strawberries back into your diet, don't add anything else, just the strawberries for a three day period. Then try another food in addition to the strawberries for three days. Try not to eat more than 2-3 pieces of fruit a day until you are really well and even beyond.

If you do notice that the foods you're reintroducing are causing reactions it doesn't mean you have to start from square one, just back off that food until you're feeling better and reintroduce it slower the next time.

The rate at which you reintroduce those foods will vary for everyone. A common mistake is to add foods back too quickly and a year later you're faced with candida once again. Don't let all that hard work go to waste!

If you follow this stage long-term, candida will become a thing of the past. This stage is like your own secret weapon to prevent you from falling under candida's sticky hands again.

Remember - slow and steady wins the race. Keep tabs on yourself by taking the Yeast Infection Evaluation Test periodically to see where you're at.

STAGE 3 FOODS

Fruits Low in Sugar	Fruits Moderate in Sugar	Fruits High in Sugar
• avocado • blueberries • blackberries • cranberries • lemons • limes • raspberries • rhubarb (technically not a fruit, but. . .ya know) • strawberries • green apples	• apples (some mod. & some high) • cantaloupe • guavas • honeydew • nectarines • papaya • peaches • watermelon	• any dried fruit • apricots • bananas • cherries • dates • figs • grapefruit • grapes • kiwi • mangoes • oranges (tend to be moldy too) • pears • pineapple • plums • pomegranates • prunes • raisins • tangerines

RECIPE INDEX

STAGE ONE

STAGE TWO

STAGE THREE

RECIPES WITHOUT XYLITOL

Made in the USA
San Bernardino, CA
23 February 2018